UNLOCKING THE BIBLE
Charts, diagrams and images

DAVID PAWSON

ANCHOR RECORDINGS

First published in Great Britain in 2017 by
Anchor Recordings Ltd

DPTT, Synegis House, 21 Crockhamwell Road,
Woodley, Reading RG5 3LE

**For David Pawson's teaching,
including DVDs and CDs, go to
www.davidpawson.com**

**FOR FREE DOWNLOADS
www.davidpawson.org**

**For further information, email
info@davidpawsonministry.org**

ISBN 978-1-911173-17-5

Printed by Lightning Source

HOW TO USE THE BOOK

Providing an overview of the unique account of God's relationship with his people in both the Old and New Testaments, *Unlocking the Bible*, by the widely respected evangelical speaker and writer David Pawson, gives a real sense of the sweep of biblical history and its implications for our lives, opening up the Word of God in a fresh and powerful way. Avoiding the small detail of verse-by-verse studies, it sets out the epic true story of God and his people. The culture, historical background and people are introduced, and the teaching is applied to the modern world.

This collection of maps, diagrams and charts is intended for use as a *supplement* to the related recorded teaching sessions by David Pawson, providing illustrations which the author has used to accompany his talks. The sessions were delivered over a period of many decades, so some of the resources, where they refer to facts which were correct at the time of first use, may no longer be up-to-date. (This would apply, for example, to the illustrations of tall buildings.) Moreover, as the images will have been used in more than one talk, or in relation to more than one Bible study, some of them are intentionally duplicated here, thus providing, as far as possible, a full and appropriately accessible record of the resources used in each teaching series.

David Pawson's talks on *Unlocking the Bible* can be found at:

www.davidpawson.org

or on the YouTube channel:

www.youtube.com/user/DavidPawsonMinistry

As indicated above, they can also be used alongside and as a supplement to the book entitled *Unlocking the Bible* which can be purchased from the links below:

Buy the ebook: **www.davidpawson.com/utbbuykindle**

Buy the book: **www.davidpawson.com/utbbuybook**

CONTENTS

THE OLD TESTAMENT

THE NEW TESTAMENT

OLD
TESTAMENT

OLD TESTAMENT OVERVIEW

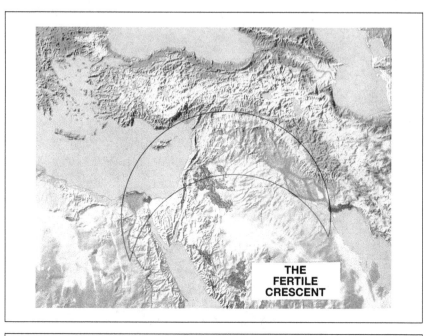

THE FERTILE CRESCENT

THE PROMISED LAND

OLD TESTAMENT OVERVIEW

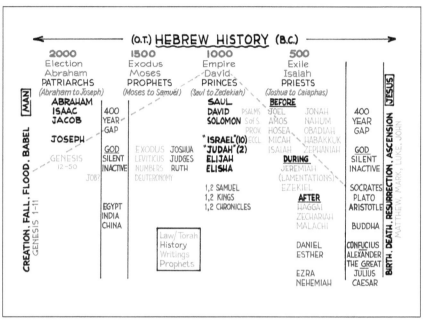

(O.T.) HEBREW HISTORY (B.C.)

2000	1500	1000	500
Election	Exodus	Empire	Exile
Abraham	Moses	David	Isaiah
PATRIARCHS	PROPHETS	PRINCES	PRIESTS
(Abraham to Joseph)	(Moses to Samuel)	(Saul to Zedekiah)	(Joshua to Caiaphas)

MAN

CREATION, FALL, FLOOD, BABEL — GENESIS 1-11

ABRAHAM
ISAAC
JACOB   400 YEAR GAP

JOSEPH

GENESIS 12-50

JOB?

GOD SILENT INACTIVE

EXODUS JOSHUA
LEVITICUS JUDGES
NUMBERS RUTH
DEUTERONOMY

EGYPT
INDIA
CHINA

Law/Torah
History
Writings
Prophets

SAUL
DAVID
SOLOMON

"ISRAEL" (10)
"JUDAH" (2)
ELIJAH
ELISHA

1,2 SAMUEL
1,2 KINGS
1,2 CHRONICLES

PSALMS
S of S.
PROV.
ECCL

BEFORE
JOEL   JONAH
AMOS   NAHUM
HOSEA   OBADIAH
MICAH   HABAKKUK
ISAIAH   ZEPHANIAH

DURING
JEREMIAH
(LAMENTATIONS)
EZEKIEL

AFTER
HAGGAI
ZECHARIAH
MALACHI

DANIEL
ESTHER

EZRA
NEHEMIAH

400 YEAR GAP

GOD SILENT INACTIVE

SOCRATES
PLATO
ARISTOTLE

BUDDHA

CONFUCIUS
ALEXANDER THE GREAT

JULIUS
CAESAR

BIRTH, DEATH, RESURRECTION, ASCENSION — JESUS

MATTHEW, MARK, LUKE, JOHN

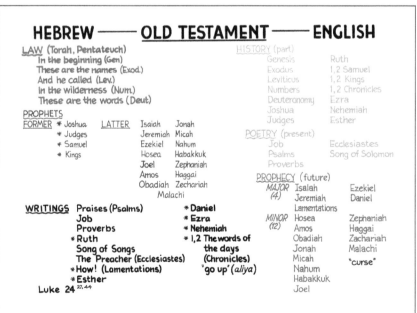

HEBREW —— OLD TESTAMENT —— ENGLISH

LAW (Torah, Pentateuch)
In the beginning (Gen)
These are the names (Exod.)
And he called (Lev.)
In the wilderness (Num.)
These are the words (Deut)

PROPHETS
FORMER * Joshua LATTER Isaiah Jonah
     * Judges   Jeremiah Micah
     * Samuel   Ezekiel Nahum
     * Kings   Hosea Habakkuk
     Joel Zephaniah
     Amos Haggai
     Obadiah Zechariah
     Malachi

WRITINGS Praises (Psalms) * Daniel
     Job   * Ezra
     Proverbs   * Nehemiah
     * Ruth   * 1,2 The words of
     Song of Songs   the days
     The Preacher (Ecclesiastes)   (Chronicles)
     * How! (Lamentations)   "go up" (aliya)
     * Esther
Luke 24 27,44

HISTORY (part)
Genesis   Ruth
Exodus   1,2 Samuel
Leviticus   1,2 Kings
Numbers   1,2 Chronicles
Deuteronomy   Ezra
Joshua   Nehemiah
Judges   Esther

POETRY (present)
Job   Ecclesiastes
Psalms   Song of Solomon
Proverbs

PROPHECY (future)
MAJOR Isaiah   Ezekiel
(4)   Jeremiah   Daniel
     Lamentations
MINOR Hosea   Zephaniah
(12)   Amos   Haggai
     Obadiah   Zechariah
     Jonah   Malachi
     Micah   "curse"
     Nahum
     Habakkuk
     Joel

OLD TESTAMENT OVERVIEW

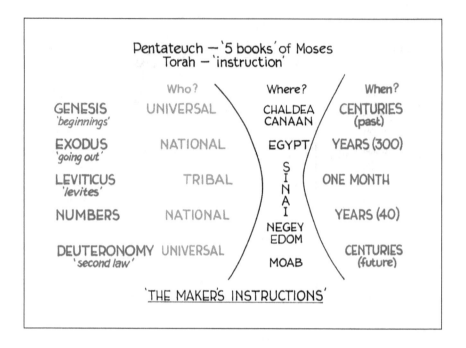

Pentateuch — '5 books' of Moses
Torah — 'instruction'

	Who?	Where?	When?
GENESIS *'beginnings'*	UNIVERSAL	CHALDEA CANAAN	CENTURIES (past)
EXODUS *'going out'*	NATIONAL	EGYPT	YEARS (300)
LEVITICUS *'levites'*	TRIBAL	S I N A I	ONE MONTH
NUMBERS	NATIONAL		YEARS (40)
DEUTERONOMY *'second law'*	UNIVERSAL	NEGEY EDOM MOAB	CENTURIES (future)

'THE MAKER'S INSTRUCTIONS'

GENESIS I – "GOD" 35 x

GOD IS PERSONAL (heart, mind, will)
        POWERFUL (10 commands obeyed)
        UNCREATED (already, always there)
        CREATIVE (imagination ⟶ variety)
        ORDERLY (symmetry, mathematics)
        SINGULAR (verbs)
        PLURAL (noun)
        GOOD (all he does because he is)
        LOVING (wants to bless those he makes)
        LIVING (active in this world)
        SPEAKING (communicates to relate)
        LIKE US (in his image)
        UNLIKE US (we can't create)
NOT | IDENTIFIED WITH | HIS CREATION
     | DEPENDENT UPON |

5

HUMAN PHILOSOPHIES

ATHEISM: no God

AGNOSTICISM: don't know

ANIMISM: spirits are gods

POLYTHEISM: many gods

DUALISM: two gods < good / bad

MONOTHEISM: one God

DEISM: Creator can't control

THEISM: Creator can control

EXISTENTIALISM: experience is god

HUMANISM: man is god

RATIONALISM: reason is god

MATERIALISM: only matter is real

MYSTICISM: only spirit is real

MONISM: matter & spirit are one

PANTHEISM: all is god

PANENTHEISM: God is in all

BIBLICAL PHILOSOPHY

TRIUNETHEISM: 3 in 1 Creator controls creatures & creation

And God said,

Let:

$$\frac{1}{r^2}\frac{\partial}{\partial r}(r^2 D_r) + \frac{1}{r\sin\theta}\frac{\partial}{\partial\theta}(D_\theta\sin\theta) + \frac{1}{r\sin\theta}\frac{\partial D_\phi}{\partial\phi} = 4\pi\rho,$$

$$\frac{1}{r^2}\frac{\partial}{\partial r}(r^2 B_r) + \frac{1}{r\sin\theta}\frac{\partial}{\partial\theta}(B_\theta\sin\theta) + \frac{1}{r\sin\theta}\frac{\partial B_\phi}{\partial\phi} = 0;$$

$$\frac{1}{r\sin\theta}\left[\frac{\partial}{\partial\theta}(E_\phi\sin\theta) - \frac{\partial E_\theta}{\partial\phi}\right] = -\frac{1}{c}\frac{\partial B_r}{\partial t},$$

$$\frac{1}{r}\left[\frac{1}{\sin\theta}\frac{\partial E_r}{\partial\phi} - \frac{\partial}{\partial r}(rE_\phi)\right] = -\frac{1}{c}\frac{\partial B_\theta}{\partial t},$$

$$\frac{1}{r}\left[\frac{\partial}{\partial r}(rE_\theta) - \frac{\partial E_r}{\partial\theta}\right] = -\frac{1}{c}\frac{\partial B_\phi}{\partial t};$$

$$\frac{1}{r\sin\theta}\left[\frac{\partial}{\partial\theta}(H_\phi\sin\theta) - \frac{\partial H_\theta}{\partial\phi}\right] = 4\pi j_r + \frac{1}{c}\frac{\partial D_r}{\partial t},$$

$$\frac{1}{r}\left[\frac{1}{\sin\theta}\frac{\partial H_r}{\partial\phi} - \frac{\partial}{\partial r}(rH_\phi)\right] = 4\pi j_\theta + \frac{1}{c}\frac{\partial D_\theta}{\partial t},$$

$$\frac{1}{r}\left[\frac{\partial}{\partial r}(rH_\theta) - \frac{\partial H_r}{\partial\theta}\right] = 4\pi j_\phi + \frac{1}{c}\frac{\partial D_\phi}{\partial t};$$

and there was light.

STYLE: NOT SCIENTIFIC (HOW?)
BUT SIMPLISTIC (WHAT?)
1. SUBJECT (GOD, WORD, SPIRIT)
2. VERBS (CREATED, MADE)
3. OBJECTS (DAYS 1-7)

STRUCTURE:

Uninhabitable	Uninhabited
GOD FORMS	GOD FILLS
Contrast	Content
1. LIGHT FROM DARKNESS	4. SUN AND MOON (+ stars)
2. SKY FROM OCEAN	5. BIRDS AND FISH
3. LAND FROM SEA (+plants)	6. ANIMALS AND HUMANS

7. DAY OFF!

LOGICAL: (simplified summary)
1. BRICKLAYER
2. CARPENTER
3. PLUMBER
4. ELECTRICIAN
5. PLASTERER
6. DECORATOR
7. HOLIDAY

CHRONOLOGICAL: (critical path analysis)
1. BRICKLAYER
2. CARPENTER
3. PLUMBER
4. ELECTRICIAN
5. PLASTERER
6. DECORATOR
7. HOLIDAYS

SCIENCE AND SCRIPTURE

1. REPUDIATE
BELIEVERS DENY SCIENCE   *UNBELIEVERS DENY SCRIPTURE*

2. SEGREGATE
SCIENCE — PHYSICAL TRUTH (WHEN? HOW?)
SCRIPTURE — SPIRITUAL TRUTH (WHO? WHY?)
WHERE IS LINE BETWEEN { *MYTH AND HISTORY?*
                           VALUES AND FACTS ?

3. INTEGRATE
TRANSITIONAL INVESTIGATIONS OF SCIENCE
TRADITIONAL INTERPRETATIONS OF SCRIPTURE
    CREATION: SPEED (6 DAYS OR OVER 4 MILLION YEARS?)
                 SEQUENCE (LIGHT BEFORE SUN, BIRDS BEFORE ANIMALS?)
                 SELECTION (NATURAL OR SUPERNATURAL?)
    MAN: DERIVATION (MINERAL OR ANIMAL?)
           DURATION (DECADES OR CENTURIES?)
           DECEASE (NATURAL OR JUDICIAL?)
    FLOOD: EXTENT (LOCAL OR UNIVERSAL?)

"DAY" (Hebrew - YOM)

I. LITERAL (earth-day)
    a. Gap
    b. Flood
    c. Antique

2. GEOLOGICAL (age-day)

3. MYTHOLOGICAL (fable-day)

4. EDUCATIONAL (school-day)
    a. Verbal
    b. Visual

5. THEOLOGICAL (God-day)

"all in a week's work"
Note length of seventh day.

GENESIS PART 3

CHAPTER ONE (1¹-2³)   CHAPTER TWO (2⁴⁻²⁵)

——— **GOD** ———

"GOD"   "LORD GOD"

ELOHIM = THREE GODS   JHVH = BEING, AM, ALWAYS

LIKE MAN   UNLIKE MAN

——— **MAN** ———

"MAN"   "ADAM" = DUSTY ("EVE" = LIVELY)

LIKE GOD   UNLIKE GOD

$\left.\begin{array}{l}\text{LIKE}\\\text{UNLIKE}\end{array}\right\}$ ANIMALS

RELATIONSHIPS

WOMAN	made | after	BELOW ⁓ SUBDUE	MAN
	from	ABOVE ⁓ SUBMIT	
↓	for	BESIDE ⁓ SUPPORT	↓
ASSIST	named by		PROVIDE
AGREE			PROTECT

ORIGIN OF MAN

a. BIBLICAL   "let us.........our image"
             "created........from dust (woman from man)"

b. HISTORICAL   Unity of human race
                Agricultural archeology

c. PRE-HISTORIC   Homo sapiens
                  Neanderthal, Peking, Java, etc.
        SCIENCE ⁓ false investigation?
        SCRIPTURE ⁓ false information?

   a. PREHISTORIC WAS BIBLICAL (ie image of God)
            Gen 1: paleolithic hunter
            Gen 2: neolithic farmer   (Adam not first man)

   b. PREHISTORIC BECAME BIBLICAL
            Did one, some, all change?
            'Sons of God and daughters of men' (Gen 6)

   c. PREHISTORIC NOT BIBLICAL
            Physical likeness, not spiritual
            Species now extinct

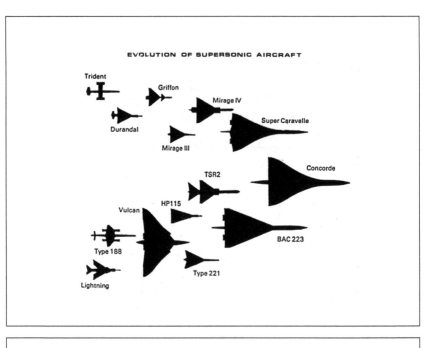

THEORY OF EVOLUTION
(TERMINOLOGY)

"VARIATION" ~ small, gradual changes in form
"SELECTION" ~ survival by suitability to environment
"NATURAL" ~ self-operating process (v. supernatural)
"MUTATION" ~ big, sudden changes in form (ie internal genes)

MICRO-EVOLUTION
    Limited development within different groups
MACRO-EVOLUTION
    Total development from single origin
"STRUGGLE" ~ survival of the fittest
  (key-word)

1. MENTAL CHOICE

CREATION	EVOLUTION
Father God	Mother nature
Personal choice	Impersonal chance
Designed purpose	Random pattern
Supernatural production	Natural process
Open situation	Closed system
Providence	Coincidence

Faith based on fact | Faith based on fancy

God free to make
man in his image

Man free to make
God in his image
imagination

2. MORAL CHOICE

CREATION	EVOLUTION
God is Lord	Man is lord
Divine authority	Human autonomy
Absolute standards	Relative situations
Duty - responsibility	Demand- rights
'Infant' dependence	'Adult' independence
Man fallen	Man rising
Salvation of weak	Survival of strong
Right is might	Might is right
Peace	War
Obedience	Indulgence
Faith, hope and love	Fatalism, helplessness and luck
Heaven	Hell

GENESIS PART 4

FLOOD SEDIMENT IN MESOPOTAMIA

ANIMALS ENTER ARK

S.S. CANBERRA

BABYLON (BABEL)

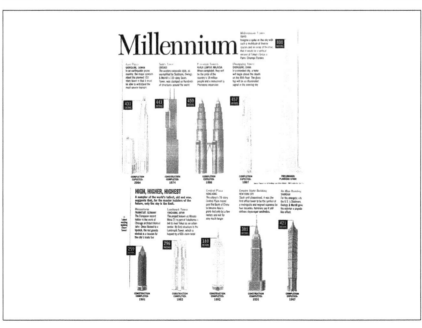

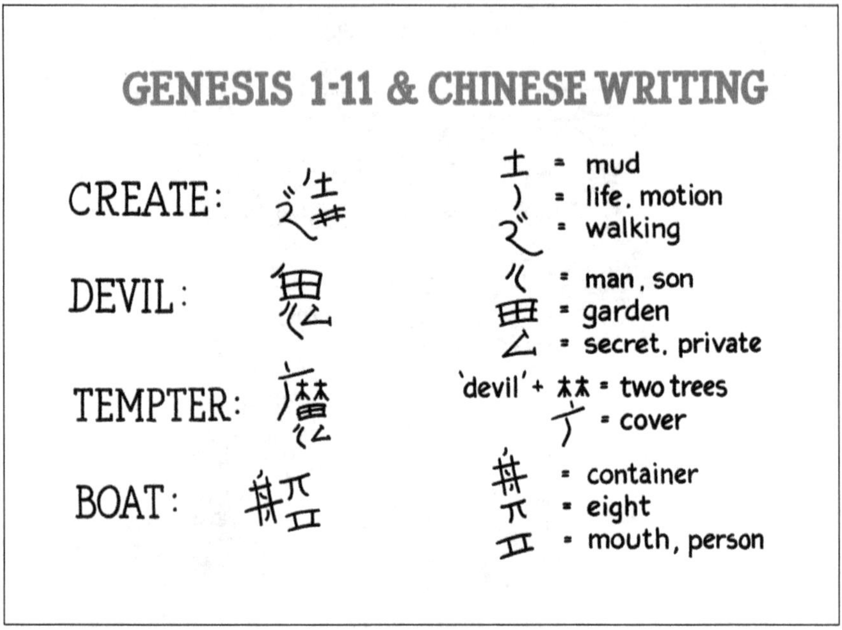

GENESIS 1-11 & CHINESE WRITING

CREATE:

DEVIL:

TEMPTER:

BOAT:

土 = mud
丿 = life, motion
辶 = walking

亻 = man, son
田 = garden
厶 = secret, private

'devil' + 林 = two trees
宀 = cover

井 = container
八 = eight
口 = mouth, person

OUTLINE OF GENESIS

1-11	12-50
Short section (1/4)	Long section (3/4)
Long Period (centuries)	Short period (years)
Many people (nations)	Few people (family)

1-2 GOOD CREATOR	**12-36 GOD OF ABRAHAM** V. LOT
DIVINE ACTIONS	**ISAAC** V. ISHMAEL
HUMAN RELATIONS	**JACOB** V. ESAU
3-11 BAD CREATURES	**37-50 JOSEPH OF GOD**
FALL	DOWN TO PRISONER
FALL OUT	UP TO PREMIER

ZIGGURAT IN UR

15

GENESIS PART 5

FIREPLACE IN UR

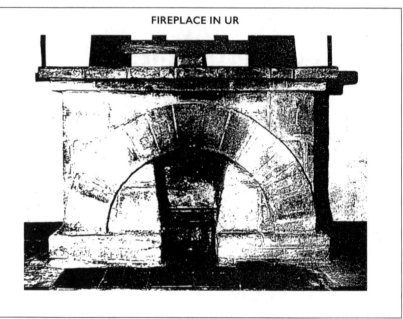

JORDAN VALLEY

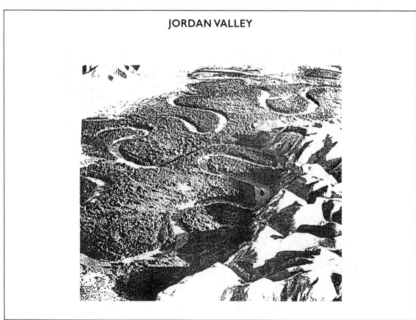

GENESIS PART 5

LOT'S WIFE

PETRA

EXODUS PART I

CHS. 1-18

**DIVINE DEEDS
GRACE
LIBERATION
FROM EGYPT
SLAVERY
REDEMPTION**

1. Multiplication and murder
   (ISRAEL)
2-4. Bulrushes and bush
   (MOSES)
5-11. Plague and pestilence
   (PHARAOH)
12-13^{16} Feast and firstborn
   (PASSOVER)
13^{17}-15^{21} Delivered and drowned
   (RED SEA)
15^{22}-18^{27} Provided and protected
   (WILDERNESS)

CHS. 19-40

**DIVINE WORDS
GRATITUDE
LEGISLATION
TO SINAI
SERVICE
RIGHTEOUSNESS**

19-24 Commandments and covenant
   (SINAI)
25-31 Specification and specialists
   (TABERNACLE)
32-34 Indulgence and intercession
   (GOLDEN CALF)
35-40 Construction and consecration
   (TABERNACLE)

RAMESSES II

EXODUS PART 1

PASSOVER

EXODUS PART 2

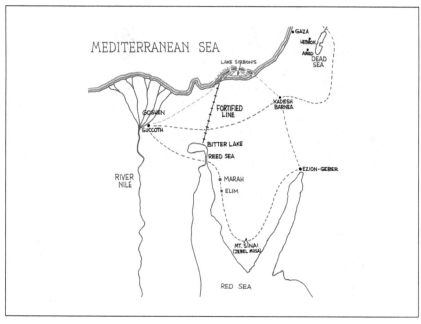

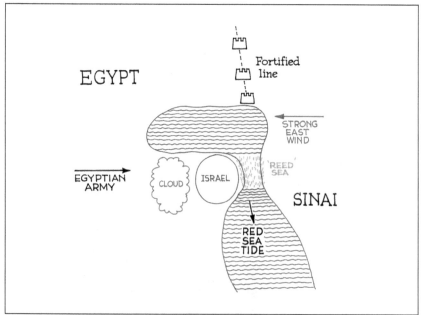

EXODUS PART 2

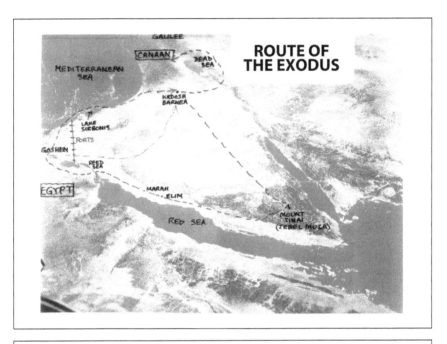

ROUTE OF THE EXODUS

CHS. 1-18	CHS. 19-40
DIVINE DEEDS	**DIVINE WORDS**
GRACE	**GRATITUDE**
LIBERATION	**LEGISLATION**
FROM EGYPT	**TO SINAI**
SLAVERY	**SERVICE**
REDEMPTION	**RIGHTEOUSNESS**

CHS. 1-18	CHS. 19-40
1. Multiplication and murder (ISRAEL)	19-24 Commandments and covenant (SINAI)
2-4. Bulrushes and bush (MOSES)	25-31 Specification and specialists (TABERNACLE)
5-11. Plague and pestilence (PHARAOH)	32-34 Indulgence and intercession (GOLDEN CALF)
12-13^{16} Feast and firstborn (PASSOVER)	35-40 Construction and consecration (TABERNACLE)
13^{17}-15^{21} Delivered and drowned (RED SEA)	
15^{22}-18^{27} Provided and protected (WILDERNESS)	

EXODUS PART 2

MARAH

ELIM

EXODUS PART 2

MT. SINAI

ISRAELITE CAMP

EXODUS PART 2

TABERNACLE (VEIL)

TABERNACLE

EXODUS PART 2

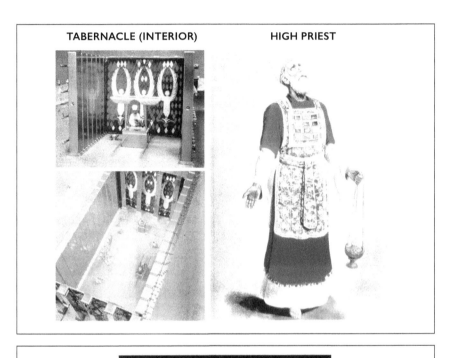

TABERNACLE (INTERIOR) **HIGH PRIEST**

GOLDEN CALF

`PENTATEUCH`- <u>5</u> books of Moses - `TORAH`- instruction

	WHO?	WHERE?	WHEN?
GENESIS *BEGINNINGS*	UNIVERSAL	CHALDEA CANAAN	CENTURIES *(PAST)*
EXODUS *GOING OUT*	NATIONAL	EGYPT	YEARS *(300)*
LEVITICUS *LEVITES*	TRIBAL	S I N A I	MONTH *(ONE)*
NUMBERS *STATISTICS*	NATIONAL		YEARS *(40)*
DEUTERONOMY *SECOND LAW*	UNIVERSAL	NEGEV EDOM MOAB	CENTURIES *(FUTURE)*

JUSTIFICATION
WAY <u>TO</u> GOD

- - - - - - - - - - - - - - -

WALK <u>WITH</u> GOD
SANCTIFICATION

1-7 OFFERINGS & SACRIFICES

8-10 PRIESTHOOD

11-15 UNCLEAN → CLEAN

16 DAY of ATONEMENT

17-22 COMMON → HOLY

23-25 WORSHIP

26-27 SANCTIONS & VOWS

OFFERINGS

GRATITUDE {	**BURNT**	*Surrender*
	MEAL	*Service*
	PEACE	*Serenity*
GUILT {	**SIN**	*Substitute*
	TRESPASS	*Satisfaction*

FEASTS

FIRST COMING *(PAST)* {
- **PASSOVER** — 15th of first month *(unleavened bread)*
- **FIRSTFRUITS** — 3 days later
- **PENTECOST** — 50 days later *(weeks)*

SECOND COMING *(FUTURE)* {
- **TRUMPETS** — 1st of seventh month
- **DAY OF ATONEMENT** — 3 days later
- **TABERNACLES** — 15-22 days later *(succoth-booths)*

REST　　**SABBATICAL** — every 7th day

RELEASE　　**JUBILEE** — every 50th year

LEVITICUS PART 1

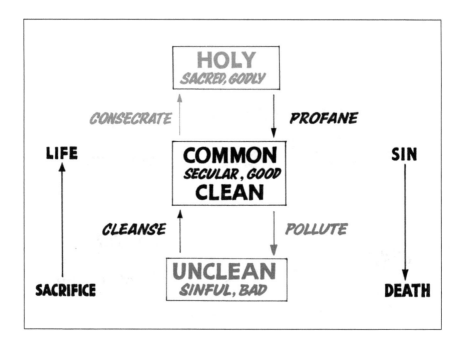

LEVITICUS PART 2

THE SCAPEGOAT

MT. ETNA

OFFERINGS

GRATITUDE {	**BURNT**	*Surrender*
	MEAL	*Service*
	PEACE	*Serenity*
GUILT {	**SIN**	*Substitute*
	TRESPASS	*Satisfaction*

NUMBERS PART I

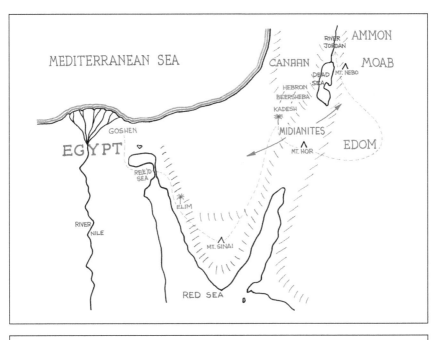

EGYPT
EXODUS 1-11
EGYPT TO SINAI
EXODUS 12-18
SINAI
EXODUS 19-40
LEVITICUS 1-27
NUMBERS 1^1-10^{10}
SINAI TO KADESH
NUMBERS 10^{11}-12^{16}
KADESH
NUMBERS 13^1-20^{21}
KADESH TO MOAB
NUMBERS 20^{22}-21^{35}
MOAB
NUMBERS 22^1-36^{13}
DEUTERONOMY 1-34

NUMBERS PART I

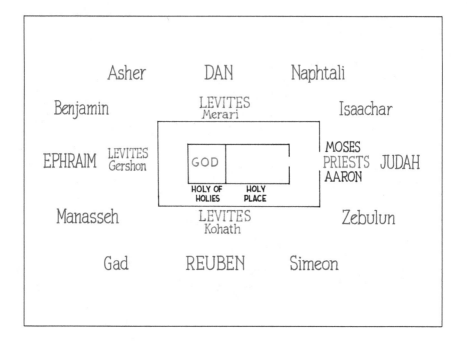

NUMBERS PART 2

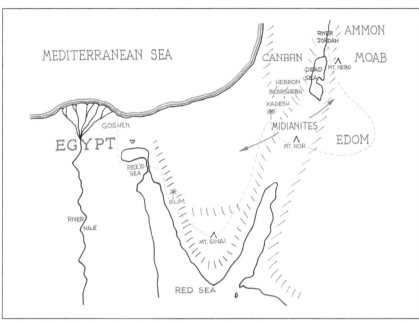

GRAPES IN CANAAN

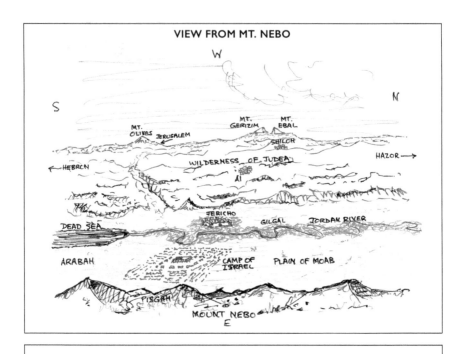

VIEW FROM MT. NEBO

SUZERAIN TREATY
(BETWEEN KING and NEW SUBJECTS)

PREAMBLE 1$^{1-5}$
HISTORICAL PROLOGUE 1^{6}-4^{49}
DECLARATION BASIC PRINCIPLES 5-11
DETAILED LEGISLATION 12-26
SANCTIONS 27-28
INVOCATION OF WITNESS 30^{19} 31^{19} 32
(USUALLY DIVINE)
PROVISION FOR CONTINUITY 31-34

CEREMONY OF RATIFICATION

DEUTERONOMY
(DEUTERO = SECOND;   NOMOS = LAW)

1. PAST: RECOLLECTION (1^1-4^{43})
a. FAITHLESSNESS CONDEMNED (1^6-3^{29})
b. FAITHFULNESS COUNSELLED (4^{1-43})

2. PRESENT: REGULATION (4^{44}-26^{19})
a. LOVE EXPRESSED (4^{44}-11^{32})
b. LAW EXPANDED (12^1-26^{19})

3. FUTURE: RETRIBUTION (27^1-34^{12})
a. COVENANT AFFIRMED (27^1-30^{20})
b. CONTINUITY ASSURED (31^1-34^{12})

OLD TESTAMENT (Hebrew)

FIRST FIVE BOOKS
- Genesis
- Exodus
- Leviticus
- Numbers
- Deuteronomy

NEXT SIX BOOKS
- Joshua
- Judges
- 1, 2 Samuel
- 1, 2 Kings

LAW (TORAH)
- PROMISE
- GRACE
- REDEMPTION
- LEGISLATION
- BLESSED

- CURSED

- COVENANT ESTABLISHED
- CAUSE

PROPHETS (FORMER)
- FULFILMENT
- GRATITUDE
- RIGHTEOUSNESS
- APPLICATION
- OBEDIENCE   Joshua
  (LAND GIVEN)

- DISOBEDIENCE
  (LAND TAKEN)   2 Kings

- COVENANT EXPRESSED
- EFFECT

'JOSHUA' – OUTLINE

1. HIS COMMISSION (1)
   a. Divine encouragement (vv. 1-9)
   b. Human enthusiasm (vv. 10-18)

2. HIS COMMAND (2-22)

   A. ENTERING (2-5)
   i. Before (2)
   ii. During (3-4)
   iii. After (5 1-12)
   iv. Captain of Lord's host (5 13-15)

   B. CONQUERING (6-12)
   i. Centre (6-8)
   ii. South (9-10)
   iii. North (11)
   iv. List of defeated kings (12)

   C. DIVIDING (13-22)
   i. East Bank (13)
   ii. West Bank (14-19)
   iii Special cities (20-21)
   iv Altar of departing tribes (22)

   3. HIS COMMITMENT (23-24)
      a. Office of leadership (23)
      b. Oath of loyalty (24)

JOSHUA PART 2

JERICHO TELL

JERICHO (FROM ABOVE)

JOSHUA PART 2

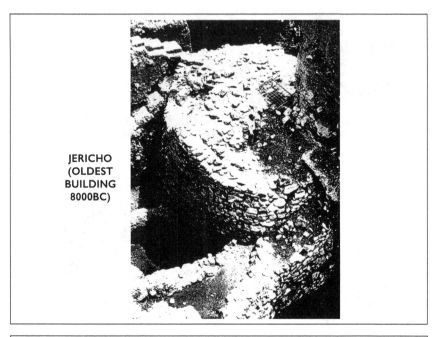

JERICHO
(OLDEST
BUILDING
8000BC)

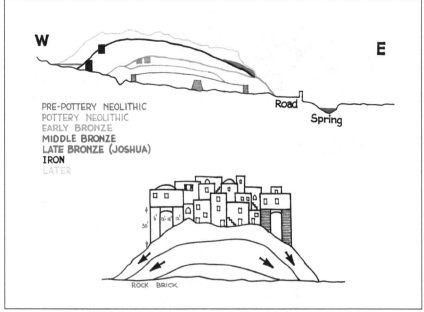

W

E

PRE-POTTERY NEOLITHIC
POTTERY NEOLITHIC
EARLY BRONZE
MIDDLE BRONZE
LATE BRONZE (JOSHUA)
IRON
LATER

Road

Spring

ROCK BRICK

AI

'JOSHUA' - OUTLINE

1. HIS COMMISSION (1)
        a. Divine encouragement (vv. 1-9)
        b. Human enthusiasm (vv. 10-18)

2. HIS COMMAND (2-22)
    A. ENTERING (2-5)   B. CONQUERING (6-12)
        i. Before (2)   i. Centre (6-8)
        ii. During (3-4)   ii. South (9-10)
        iii. After (5 1-12)   iii. North (11)
        iv. Captain of Lord's host (5 13-15)   iv. List of defeated kings (12)

                    C. DIVIDING (13-22)
                        i. East Bank (13)
                        ii. West Bank (14-19)
                        iii Special cities (20-21)
                        iv Altar of departing tribes (22)

            3. HIS COMMITMENT (23-24)
                a. Office of leadership (23)
                b. Oath of loyalty (24)

JOSHUA PART 2

THE VALLEY OF AIJALON

THE
PROMISED
LAND

A. DIVINE INTERVENTION
Without him, they couldn't have done it.
1. HIS WORDS
2. HIS DEEDS

B. HUMAN CO-OPERATION
Without them, he wouldn't have done it.
1. THEIR ATTITUDE ⎫
   Confidence   ⎬ JERICHO
2. THEIR ACTION ⎪
   Obedience   ⎭

WRONG ATTITUDE ⎫
   Self-confidence ⎬ AI
WRONG ACTION ⎪
   Disobedience ⎭

Defeated by superior troops (7)
Deceived by subtle tricks (9)
Divided by supposed treachery (22)

HISTORY —— *PERSONALITIES*
PEOPLES
PATTERNS
PURPOSE

HUMAN FUTILITY (Judges)

DIVINE FULFILMENT (Ruth)

PAST   PRESENT   FUTURE

OPPRESSORS   DELIVERERS (Judges)

OPPRESSORS	DELIVERERS
KING OF JERICHO	OTHNIEL
KING OF MOAB	EHUD
AMMONITES	SHAMGAR
AMALEKITES	* DEBORAH/BARAK
* PHILISTINES	** GIDEON
KING OF HAZOR	TOLA
MIDIANITES +EASTERNS	JAIR
AMALEKITES	JEPHTHAH
* PHILISTINES	IBZAN
AMMONITES	ELON
AMMONITES	ABDON
* PHILISTINES	*** SAMSON

Human weakness : divine strength

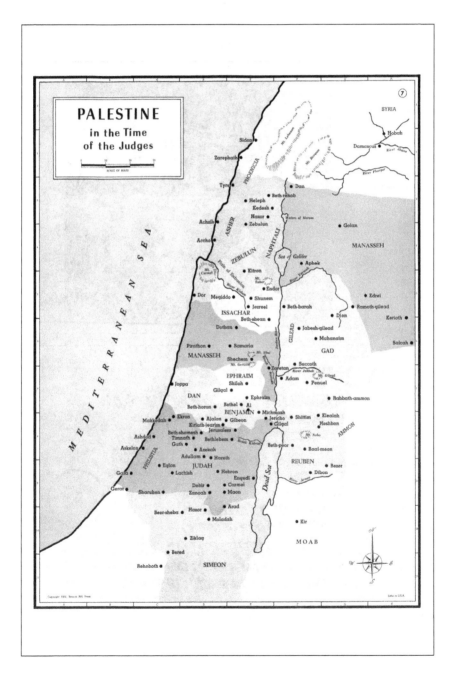

PALESTINE
in the Time
of the Judges

SCALE OF MILES

GIDEON'S
SPRING
(SPRING OF
HAROD)

OUTLINE of JUDGES:

A. INEXCUSABLE COMPROMISE (1.1 - 3.6)
   1. ALLOWANCES *(vulnerable valleys)*
   2. ALLIANCES *(mixed marriages)*

B. INCORRIGIBLE CONDUCT (3.7 - 16.31)
   1. SEDITION *(by the people)*
   2. SUBJECTION *(to an enemy)*
   3. SUPPLICATION *(to the Lord)*
   4. SALVATION *(by a deliverer)*

C. INEVITABLE CORRUPTION (17.1 - 21.25)
   1. IDOLATRY *(in the north)*: DAN
   2. IMMORALITY *(in the south)*: BENJAMIN

   No king in those days
   Did right in own eyes

JUDGES & RUTH PART 2

BETHLEHEM

FIELDS OF BOAZ

OUTLINE OF RUTH:

A. TWO INSEPARABLE WOMEN

1. MOTHER-IN-LAW'S LOSS

2. DAUGHTER-IN-LAW'S LOYALTY

B. TWO INFLUENTIAL MEN

1. REDEEMER KINSMAN'S LOVE

2. ROYAL KING'S LINE

Judges — bad Benjamin — Saul ⎫
Ruth — good Bethlehem — David ⎭ Samuel

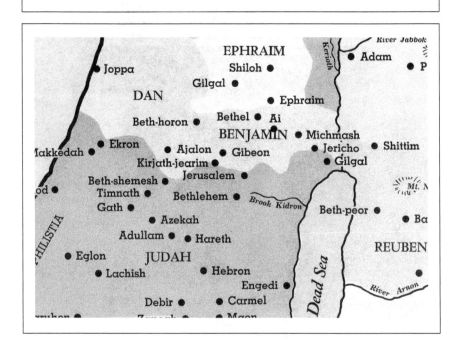

I SAMUEL

A. SAMUEL : LAST JUDGE (1-12)

1. HANNAH ~ anxious wife (1-2a)
2. ELI ~ ailing priest (2b-3)
3. ISRAEL ~ arrogant army (4-7)
4. SAUL ~ anointed king (8-12)

B. SAUL : FIRST KING (13-31)

1. JONATHAN ~ adventurous son (13-14a)
2. SAMUEL ~ angry prophet (14b-15)
3. DAVID ~ apparent rival (16-26)
   a. Simple shepherd ⎫
   b. Skilled musician ⎬ IN
   c. Superb warrior   ⎭
   d. Suspected courtier ⎫
   e. Stalked outlaw   ⎬ OUT
   f. Soldiering exile   ⎭
4. PHILISTINES ~ aggressive foe (27-31)

TEMPLE AT SHILOH

1 & 2 SAMUEL PART 1

EIN GEDI

BETH SHAN
(BETH SHEAN)

Ⅱ SAMUEL

C. DAVID: BEST KING (1-31)

1. TRIUMPHANT ASCENT (1-9)
  a. Single tribe
  b. Settled nation } UP
  c. Sizeable empire

2. TRAGIC DESCENT (10-20)
  a. Disgraced man
  b. Disintegrated family } DOWN
  c. Discontented people

Epilogue (21-24)

DAVIDS LIFE
1. IN
2. OUT } BEFORE REIGN
3. UP
4. DOWN } AFTER REIGN

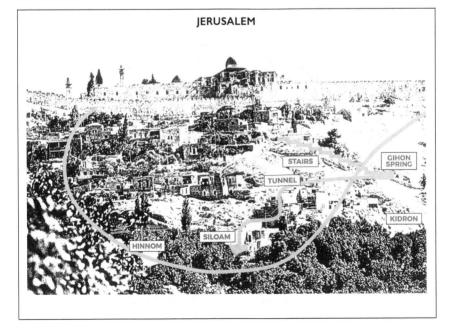

JERUSALEM

STAIRS
GIHON SPRING
TUNNEL
KIDRON
HINNOM
SILOAM

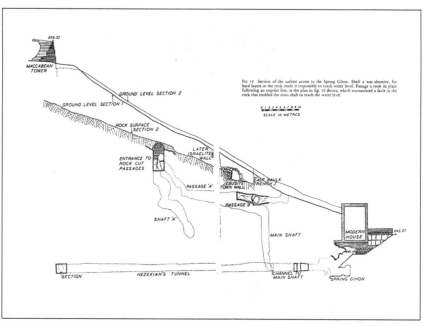

Fig 17 Section of the earliest access to the Spring Gihon. Shaft A was abortive, for hard layers in the rock made it impossible to reach water level. Passage A took its place following an angular line, as the plan in fig. 16 shows, which encountered a fault in the rock that enabled the main shaft to reach the water level

HEZEKIAH'S TUNNEL (THE SILOAM TUNNEL)

SAMUEL'S TOMB

II SAMUEL

C. DAVID: BEST KING (1-31)

I. TRIUMPHANT ASCENT (1-9)

a. Single tribe ⎫
b. Settled nation ⎬ UP
c. Sizeable empire ⎭

2. TRAGIC DESCENT (10-20)

a. Disgraced man ⎫
b. Disintegrated family ⎬ DOWN
c. Discontented people ⎭

Epilogue (21-24)

DAVIDS LIFE

1. IN ⎫
2. OUT ⎬ BEFORE REIGN

3. UP ⎫
4. DOWN ⎬ AFTER REIGN

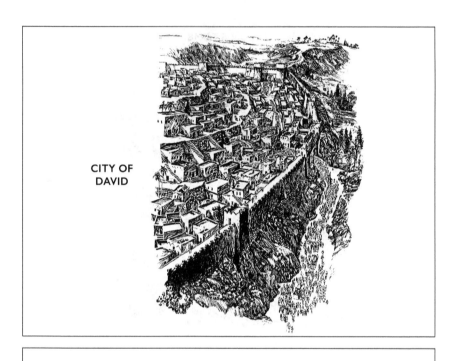

CITY OF DAVID

O. T. NARRATIVE
LEVELS OF STUDY

I. ANECDOTAL (interesting stories)
a. CHILDREN
b. ADULTS

2. DEVOTIONAL (personal messages)
a. GUIDANCE
b. COMFORT

3. BIOGRAPHICAL (character studies)
a. INDIVIDUAL
b. SOCIAL

4. HISTORICAL (national development)
a. LEADERSHIP
b. STRUCTURE

5. CRITICAL (possible errors)
a. 'LOWER' - text
b. 'HIGHER' - context

6. THEOLOGICAL (providential over-ruling)
a. JUSTICE - retribution
b. MERCY - redemption

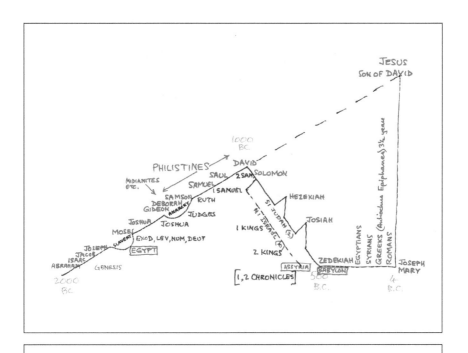

HISTORY OF ISRAEL

THREE PHASES, LED BY:

PROPHETS ~ Moses to Samuel
KINGS ~ Saul to Zedekiah
PRIESTS ~ Zerubbabel to Caiaphas

"KINGDOM(S) OF ISRAEL"
COVERED BY FOUR BOOKS

{ I SAMUEL ~ Samuel to David   { I KINGS ~ Solomon to Ahab
{ II SAMUEL ~ David   { II KINGS ~ Ahab to Zedekiah

TWO BOOKS IN HEBREW
FOUR BOOKS IN GREEK (LXX) "Kingdoms"

IN HEBREW SCRIPTURES
NOT 'HISTORY'
BUT 'PROPHECY' (Law, Prophets, Writings)
"FORMER PROPHETS"
(JOSHUA, JUDGES, SAMUEL, KINGS)
"LATTER PROPHETS"
(ISAIAH, JEREMIAH, EZEKIEL + TWELVE)

KINGDOM OF ISRAEL

1. UNITED KINGDOM

    SAUL   40   (I Samuel)

    DAVID   40   (II Samuel)

    SOLOMON 40   (I Kings 1-10)

2. DIVIDED KINGDOM

    JUDAH ~ 2 TRIBES IN SOUTH

    ISRAEL ~ 10 TRIBES IN NORTH

    WAR   80 (I 12-16)

    PEACE 80 (I 16 - II 10)   ELIJAH (I 17 - II 2)

    WAR   50 (II 11 - 17)   ELISHA (I 19 - II 9)

      ISRAEL TO ASSYRIA 721 BC

3. SINGLE KINGDOM

    JUDAH ("Jew") 140 (II 18-25)

    JUDAH TO BABYLON 587 BC.

1 & 2 KINGS PART 2

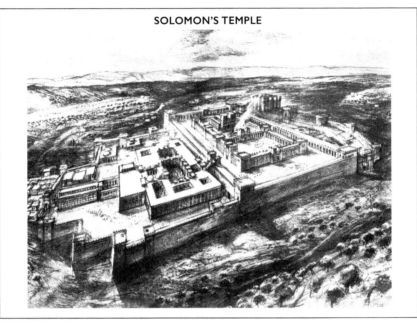

SOLOMON'S TEMPLE

QUARRY CAVE UNDER

KINGS

ISRAEL (N.10)   JUDAH (S.2)

SYNCHRONISED

DATE OF ACCESSION ————	DATE OF ACCESSION
NAME OF CAPITAL	AGE AT ACCESSION
LENGTH OF REIGN ————	LENGTH OF REIGN
JUDGEMENT (EVIL)	NAME OF MOTHER
NAME OF FATHER	JUDGEMENT (GOOD or EVIL)
SOURCE REFERENCE ————	SOURCE REFERENCE
DEATH ————	DEATH AND BURIAL
SON (UNLESS USURPER) ————	SON (SUCCESSOR)

compared to Jereboam   compared to David

NORTH "ISRAEL" (10)   SOUTH "JUDAH" (2)

Prophets	Kings	Kings	Prophets
AHIJAH	JEREBOAM	REHEBOAM	SHEMAIAH
JEHU	NADAB BA'ASHA	ABIJAM ASA	
	ELAH ZIMRI OMRI		
ELIJAH MICAIAH	AHAB AHAZIAH JEHORAM	JEHOSHOPHAT JEHORAM	OBADIAH
ELISHA	JEHU	AHAZIAH	
	JEHOAHAZ JEHOASH	ATHALIAH JOASH	JOEL
JONAH AMOS	JEREBOAM II ZECHARIAH	AMAZIAH UZZIAH	
	SHALLUM MENAHEM		
HOSEA	PEKAHIAH PEKAH	JOTHAM	ISAIAH MICAH
	HOSHEA	AHAZ	
	721 BC.	HEZEKIAH MANASSEH	
Very Good		AMON	NAHUM
Good		JOSIAH	JEREMIAH
Bad		JEHOAHAZ JEHOACHIM	ZEPHANIAH HABAKKUK
Very Bad		JEHOACHIN ZEDEKIAH	DANIEL
Queen		587 BC.	EZEKIEL

1 & 2 CHRONICLES

HEBREW —— OLD TESTAMENT —— ENGLISH

HEBREW	OLD TESTAMENT	ENGLISH
LAW (Torah, Pentateuch)	* Esther	**POETRY** (present)
In the beginning (Gen)	* Daniel	* Job * Psalms
These are the names (Exod)	* Ezra	* Proverbs * Ecclesiastes
And he called (Lev)	* Nehemiah	* Song of Solomon
In the wilderness (Num)	* 1,2 The words of the days	**PROPHECY** (future)
These are the words (Deut)	(Chronicles)	MAJOR Isaiah
PROPHETS	(Luke 24 27,44) "go up" (aliya)	(4) Jeremiah
FORMER * Joshua * Judges	**HISTORY** (past)	Lamentations
* Samuel (1) * Kings (1)	* Genesis	Ezekiel
LATTER Isaiah Jeremiah	* Exodus	Daniel
Ezekiel Hosea	* Leviticus	MINOR Hosea
Joel Amos	* Numbers	(12) Joel
Obadiah Jonah	* Deuteronomy	Amos
Micah Nahum	* Joshua	Obadiah
Habakkuk Zephaniah	* Judges	Jonah
Haggai Zechariah	* Ruth	Micah
Malachi	* 1,2 Samuel	Nahum
WRITINGS	* 1,2 Kings	Habakkuk
* Praises (Psalms)	* 1,2 Chronicles	Zepaniah
* Job	* Ezra	Haggai
* Proverbs	Nehemiah	Zechariah
* Ruth	Esther	Malachi
* Song of Songs		"curse"
* The Preacher (Ecclesiastes)		
* How (Lamentations)		

SELECTION	CONNECTION	EVALUATION
SAMUEL/KINGS		**CHRONICLES**
500 years		Starts earlier, finishes later
Written soon after events		Written long after events
Political history		Religious history
Prophetic viewpoint		Priestly viewpoint
Northern ⎫ kings Southern ⎭		Southern kings
Human failings		Divine faithfulness
Royal vices		Royal virtues
Negative		Positive
Moral ~ righteousness		Spiritual ~ ritual
PROPHET		PRIEST

1 & 2 CHRONICLES

OUTLINE	THEME
I THE GODLY KING	**RETURNING EXILES**
1-9 ADAM to SAUL First king of Israel 10-29 DAVID and the ARK Best king of Israel	_WHO_ THEY WERE ~ A ROOTED PEOPLE
II THE GODLY KINGS	_WHAT_ THEY WERE ~ A ROYAL PEOPLE
1-9 SOLOMON and the TEMPLE Last king of Israel 10-36 JEREBOAM to ZEDEKIAH Best kings of Judah Last king of Judah THRONE and TEMPLE	_WHY_ THEY WERE ~ A RELIGIOUS PEOPLE

TWO EXILES
1. 'ISRAEL' (10 TRIBES) ——→ ASSYRIA 721
2. 'JUDAH' (2 TRIBES) ——→ BABYLON 586
   (inc. BENJAMIN)
   "Jew"

THREE DEPORTATIONS
1. COURT (DANIEL) 606
2. CRAFTSMEN (EZEKIEL) 597
3. REST   586   NEBUCHADNEZZAR

THREE RETURNS   PERSIA
1. ZERUBBABEL (50,000) 537   CYRUS
   JUDAH, BENJAMIN   DARIUS I
2. EZRA (1800) 458   (XERXES)
   PRIESTS, FEW LEVITES   } ARTAXERXES I
3. NEHEMIAH 444   )

(10 tribes drift back later)

70 YEARS

EZRA	NEHEMIAH
1-2 RETURN I	**1-2** RETURN III
ab	ab
3-6 REBUILD	**3-7** REBUILD
abc	abc
7-8 RETURN II	**8-10** RENEW
abc	abc
9-10 REFORM	**11-13** REFORM
ab	ab

Ch. 9. Prayer of confession

EZRA & NEHEMIAH PART I

EZRA
OUTLINE OF BOOK

1. RETURN I (1-2)
a. CYRUS: decree to build temple (1)
b. ZERUBBABEL: and co. 'go up' (2)

2. REBUILD (3-6)
a. JESHUA: altar & temple foundation (3)
b. ARTAXERXES: letter received (4)
c. DARIUS: letter received & sent (5-6)

3. RETURN II (7-8)
a. EZRA: and co. 'go up' (7a)
b. ARTAXERXES: letter sent (7b)
c. LEVITES: 'go up' (8)

4. REFORM (9-10)
a. Private intercession (9)
b. Public confession (10)

EZRA & NEHEMIAH PART 2

NEHEMIAH
OUTLINE OF BOOK

1. **RETURN Ⅲ (1-2)**
   a. SAD INFORMATION (1)
   b. SECRET INSPECTION (2)

2. **REBUILD (3-7)**
   a. ERECTING DEFENCES (3)
   b. ENCOUNTERING DIFFICULTIES (4-6)
      i. External opposition.   ii. Internal exploitation
   c. ENLISTING DESCENDANTS (7)

3. **RENEW (8-10)**
   a. SCRIPTURE COMMUNICATED (8)
   b. SIN CONFESSED (9)
   c. SUBMISSION COVENANTED (10)

4. **REFORM (11-13)**
   a. SUFFICIENT QUANTITY (11)
   b. SPIRITUAL QUALITY (12-13)
      i. Misappropriated funds   iii. Mixed marriages
      ii. Desecrated sabbaths   iv. Neglected duties

ORIGINAL JERUSALEM

EZRA & NEHEMIAH PART 2

RIDGE OF JERUSALEM

RIDGE OF
JERUSALEM

EZRA & NEHEMIAH PART 2

NEHEMIAH'S WALL

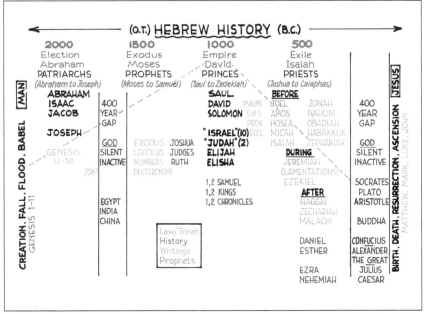

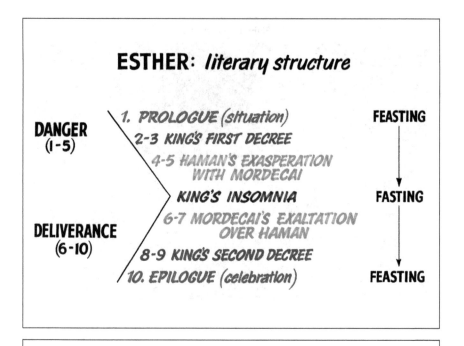

ESTHER: *literary structure*

DANGER (1-5)

1. PROLOGUE *(situation)* — FEASTING
2-3 KING'S FIRST DECREE
4-5 HAMAN'S EXASPERATION WITH MORDECAI

KING'S INSOMNIA — FASTING

DELIVERANCE (6-10)

6-7 MORDECAI'S EXALTATION OVER HAMAN
8-9 KING'S SECOND DECREE
10. EPILOGUE *(celebration)* — FEASTING

ACROSTICS IN ESTHER

1.20	5.4	5.13	7.7	7.5
DUE	LET	YET	FOR	WHERE
RESPECT	OUR	I	HE	DWELLETH
OUR	ROYAL	AM	SAW	THE ENEMY
LADIES	DINNER	SAD	THAT	THAT DARETH
SHALL	THIS	FOR	THERE	PRESUME
GIVE	DAY	NO	WAS	IN
TO	BE	AVAIL	EVIL	HIS
THEIR	GRACED	IS	TO	HEART
HUSBANDS,	BY	ALL	FEAR	TO
BOTH	KING	THIS	DETERMINED	DO
TO	AND	TO	AGAINST	THIS
GREAT	HAMAN	ME	HIM	THING
AND			BY	?
SMALL			THE	
			KING	
HVHJ	**JHVH**	**HVHJ**	**JHVH**	**EHYH**
BACKWARD GENTILE SPEAKS ABOUT QUEEN	*FORWARD JEW SPEAKS BY QUEEN*	*BACKWARD GENTILE SPEAKS BY HAMAN*	*FORWARD JEW WRITES ABOUT HAMAN*	*BACKWARD GENTILE SPEAKS - I AM (EXOD.3.15)*

STRUCTURE OF JOB

A. PROLOGUE (1-2) prose
   Two rounds: GOD and SATAN
B. DIALOGUE (3-42^6) poetry
   1. HUMAN (3-37)
      a. ELIPHAZ, BILDAD, ZOPHAR (3-31)
         i. Round 1 (3-14)
         ii Round 2 (15-21)
         iii Round 3 (22-31)
      b. ELIHU (32-37)
         A monologue!
   2. DIVINE (38-42^6)
         i. Round 1 (38-39)
         ii. Round 2 (40-42^6)
C. EPILOGUE (42$^{7-17}$)
   Final round: GOD and JOB

JOB'S THREE 'FRIENDS'

ELIPHAZ   BILDAD   ZOPHAR

RIGHTEOUS PROSPER

WICKED SUFFER

GOD'S   GOD'S   GOD'S
TRANSCENDENCE OMNIPOTENCE OMNISCIENCE

HEBREW POETRY

"PARALLELISM" Thought-rhyme
Balance of SENSE, not SOUND

1. SYNONYMOUS   Same thought - different words

a. SIMPLY REPEATED

"Where can I go from your spirit?"
"Where can I flee from your presence?"

b. TAKEN FURTHER

"O Lord, do not rebuke me in your anger,
Or discipline me in your wrath
Be merciful to me, O Lord, for I am faint,
O Lord, heal me, for my bones are in agony."

2. ANTITHETIC   Opposite thought

"Those who sow in tears
Will reap with songs of joy.
He who goes out reaping, carrying seed to sow,
Will return with songs of joy, carrying sheaves with him."

3. SYNTHETIC   Added thought

"The Lord is my shepherd,
I shall not want;
He makes me lie down in green pastures
He leads me beside still waters."

PSALMS

BOOKS:

				DIVINE NAMES	
				YAHWEH	ELOHIM
I	1-41	(41)		272	15
II	42-72	(30)		74	207
III	73-89	(16)		13	36
IV	90-106	(16)		} 339	7
V	107-150	(43)			

AUTHORS

DAVID — most in I and II, some in V
SONS OF KORAH — in II (42-49) and III
SONS OF ASAPH — in III (73-83)
ANONYMOUS — some in IV, most in V
MOSES — one in IV (90)

EIN GEDI

MASADA

PSALMS

GROUPS: ## **TYPES:**

22-24 : Cross, crook & crown   LAMENT (most)
96-99 : God is king   GRATITUDE (many)
113-118 : Hallel (Passover)   PENITENCE (few)
120-134 : Songs of ascent
146-150 : Hallelujah!

SPECIAL CATEGORIES:

ROYAL
MESSIANIC
WISDOM
'IMPRECATORY'

OUTLINE OF PROVERBS

[PROLOGUE 1^{1-7}]

ADVICE TO YOUTH (1^8-9^{18})
FROM A FATHER ABOUT BAD WOMEN

PROVERBS OF SOLOMON (10^1-22^{16})
COLLECTED BY HIMSELF

WORDS OF THE WISE (22^{17}-23^{14})
THIRTY SAYINGS

ADVICE TO YOUTH (23^{15}-24^{22})

WORDS OF THE WISE (24^{23-34})
SIX SAYINGS

PROVERBS OF SOLOMON (25^1-29^{27})
COPIED BY HEZEKIAH

[AGUR 30^{1-33}]

ADVICE TO YOUTH (31^{1-31})
FROM A MOTHER ABOUT GOOD WOMEN

ADVICE TO YOUTH (1^8-9^{18})
FROM A FATHER ABOUT BAD WOMEN

1. DO: obey your parents (1^{8-9})

　　seek & get wisdom (1^{20}-3^{26}; 4^{1-13}; 8^1-9^{12})

　　be kind to others (3^{27-35})

　　keep your heart (4^{23-27})

　　be faithful to your spouse (5^{15-23})

2. DON'T: get into bad company (1^{10-19}; 4^{14-22})

　　commit adultery (5^{1-14}; 6^{20}-7^{27})

　　take out loans (6^{1-5})

　　be lazy (6^{6-19})

　　befriend foolish women (9^{13-18})

PROVERBS OF SOLOMON (10^1-22^{16})
COLLECTED BY HIMSELF

1. CONTRAST – godly & wicked lives (10^1-15^{33})

2. CONTENT – godly life (16^1-22^{16})

PROVERBS OF SOLOMON (25^1-29^{27})
COPIED BY HEZEKIAH

1. RELATIONSHIPS with kings (25^{1-7})

　　　　　　　neighbours (25^{8-20})

　　　　　　　enemies (25^{21-24})

　　　　　　　yourself (25^{25-28})

　　　　　　　fools (26^{1-12})

　　　　　　　sluggards (26^{13-16})

　　　　　　　gossips (26^{17-28})

2. RIGHTEOUSNESS (27^1-29^{27})

ADVICE TO YOUTH (31^{1-31})
FROM A MOTHER ABOUT GOOD WOMEN

1. King of a nation (31^{1-9})

2. Queen of a home (31^{10-31})

GOD IS SOVEREIGN,
SETS THE SEASONS:
DATE OF BIRTHDAY,
DAY OF DEATH.
TIME FOR PLANTING,
TIME FOR REAPING;
TIME FOR KILLING,
TIME TO HEAL.

TIME FOR WRECKING,
TIME FOR BUILDING;
TIME FOR SORROW,
TIME FOR JOY;
TIME FOR MOURNING,
TIME FOR DANCING;
TIME FOR KISSING,
TIME TO STOP!

TIME FOR FINDING,
TIME FOR LOSING;
TIME FOR SAVING,
TIME FOR WASTE;
TIME FOR TEARING,
TIME FOR MENDING;
TIME FOR SILENCE,
TIME TO TALK.

TIME FOR LOVING,
TIME FOR HATING;
TIME FOR FIGHTING,
TIME FOR PEACE.
HAVE YOUR FUN, THEN,
BUT REMEMBER....
GOD IS SOVEREIGN;
HE DECREES.

ISAIAH PART I

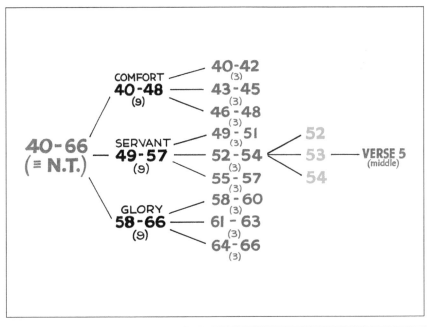

COMFORT
40-48
(9)
    40-42 (3)
    43-45 (3)
    46-48 (3)

40-66
(≡ N.T.)

SERVANT
49-57
(9)
    49-51 (3)
    52-54 (3)
    55-57 (3)

52
53 —— **VERSE 5** (middle)
54

GLORY
58-66
(9)
    58-60 (3)
    61-63 (3)
    64-66 (3)

SINS AS SCARLET

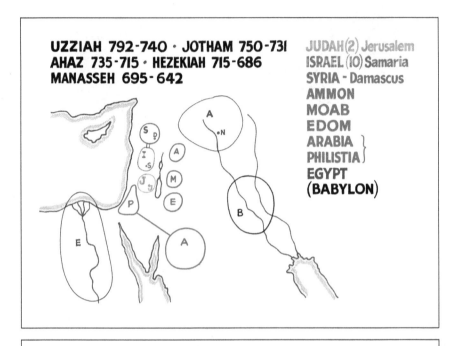

UZZIAH 792-740 · JOTHAM 750-731
AHAZ 735-715 · HEZEKIAH 715-686
MANASSEH 695-642

JUDAH(2) Jerusalem
ISRAEL (10) Samaria
SYRIA - Damascus
AMMON
MOAB
EDOM
ARABIA }
PHILISTIA }
EGYPT
(BABYLON)

KINGS · CHARACTER · BATTLES · ALLIANCES · EVENTS

KINGS	CHARACTER	BATTLES	ALLIANCES	EVENTS
UZZIAH 52	GOOD BAD	PHILISTIA ARABIA WON · ASSYRIA LOST		Leprosy AMOS N
JOTHAM 19	GOOD	AMMON WON · ISRAEL SYRIA WON	ASSYRIA	"Immanuel"
AHAZ 20	BAD	EDOM LOST · PHILISTIA LOST · ASSYRIA LOST		HOSEA N · Samaria falls } 721 Israel ends }
HEZEKIAH 29	GOOD	PHILISTIA WON · ASSYRIA WON	EGYPT	Water tunnel chs 36-39
MANASSEH 53	BAD	ASSYRIA LOST		Isaiah killed

ISAIAH PART 1

UZZIAH'S TOMB

SENNACHERIB KING OF THE ASSYRIANS

ISAIAH PART I

HEZEKIAH'S TUNNEL (THE SILOAM TUNNEL)

SILOAM INSCRIPTION

ISAIAH PART I

ASSYRIAN TROOPS

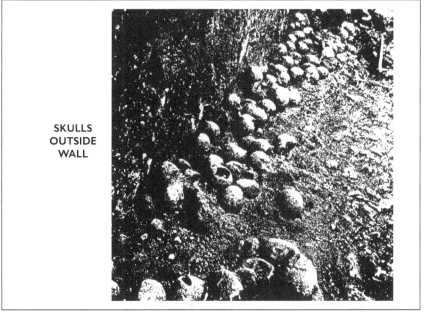

SKULLS OUTSIDE WALL

PART I (1-39 ≡ O.T.)

MORE BAD NEWS
HUMAN ACTIVITY
SIN AND RETRIBUTION
JUSTICE
CONFRONTING
GOD OF ISRAEL
NATIONAL
ISRAEL & NEIGHBOURS
GOD-FIRE
HAND UPRAISED TO STRIKE
CURSES (WOE)
'STRANGE WORK'
JEWS
ASSYRIA ------- (chs 36-39) -------
BEFORE EXILE (PRESENT)

PART II (40-66 ≡ N.T.)

MORE GOOD NEWS
DIVINE ACTIVITY
SALVATION AND REDEMPTION
MERCY
COMFORTING
CREATOR OF UNIVERSE
INTERNATIONAL
ISRAEL & NATIONS
GOD-FATHER
ARM OUTSTRETCHED TO SAVE
BLESSINGS
'GOOD TIDINGS'
GENTILES
BABYLON
AFTER EXILE (FUTURE)

JERUSALEM JEWELRY

PART I (1-39)

1-10 REPROOF : JUDAH
JERUSALEM
11-12 COMING GLORY
13-23 JUDGEMENT: OTHER
NATIONS
24-34 JUDGEMENT: SAMARIA
JUDAH
35 COMING GLORY
36-39 ASSYRIA/BABYLON

BAD NEWS	GOOD NEWS
DISOBEDIENCE	REMNANT
DISCIPLINE	RETURN
DISASTER	REIGN *
DEJECTION	REJOICING

PART II (40-66)

40-48   COMFORT
49-57   SALVATION
58-66   GLORY

"US" { GOD
SERVANT (SUFFERING) *
SPIRIT

FUTURE: JERUSALEM
NATIONS
UNIVERSE

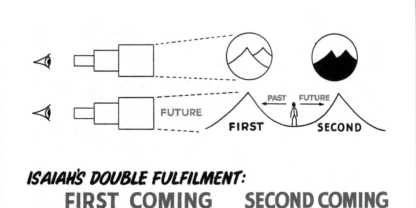

ISAIAH'S DOUBLE FULFILMENT:

FIRST COMING   SECOND COMING
'a servant shall suffer'   *'a king shall reign'*
(PART II)   *(PART I)*

JEREMIAH

I. THE MOMENT

MANASSEH	BIRTH
AMON	BOYHOOD
JOSIAH	
JEHOAHAZ	JEREMIAH
JEHOIAKIM	PROPHESIED
JEHOIAKIN	
ZEDEKIAH	

2. THE MAN
- PRIEST
- PROPHET
- POET

3. THE METHOD
- SPEAKING
- ACTING
- WRITING

4. THE MESSAGE

LIKE OTHERS
- *a. APOSTATE PEOPLE*
- *b. IMPENDING DISASTER*
- *c. ULTIMATE RESTORATION*
- *d. PUNISHED ENEMIES*

UNLIKE OTHERS
- *a. SPIRITUAL*
- *b. INDIVIDUAL*
- *c. POLITICAL*

5. THE MALTREATMENT

6. THE MISERY
THE 'WEEPING PROPHET'
LAMENTATIONS

JEREMIAH
OUTLINE

PROLOGUE (1)
PERSONAL CALL

A. SINNING NATION (2-45)
1. IMMEDIATE RETRIBUTION (2-20)
627-605 BC. *MAINLY POETRY*
BABYLON DESTROYS ASSYRIA · DEFEATS EGYPT

2. ULTIMATE RESTORATION (21-45)
605-585 BC. *MAINLY PROSE*
BABYLON DEPORTS JUDAH · DEVASTATES JERUSALEM

B. SURROUNDING NATIONS (46-51)

EPILOGUE (52)
NATIONAL CATASTROPHE

LAMENTATIONS

LAMENTATIONS

I CATASTROPHE
   'SHE'
   Acrostic - 22 verses (1 per letter) 3 lines each

II CAUSE
    'HE'
   Acrostic - 22 verses (1 per letter) 3 lines each

III CURE
    'I'
   Acrostic - 66 verses (3 per letter) 3 lines each

IV CONSEQUENCES
    'THEY'
   Acrostic - 22 verses (1 per letter) 2 lines each

V CRY
    'WE'
   Non-Acrostic - 22 verses 3 lines each

DATE B.C.	JUDAH (2)		EZEKIEL
	KINGS	*PROPHETS*	
	JOSIAH (640-609)	JEREMIAH (627-580)	BORN (623)
	JEHOAHAZ (609)	HABAKKUK (609)	
	JEHOIAKIM (609-597)	DANIEL (605-530)	TAKEN (597)
597	*FIRST DEPORTATION*		
	JEHOIAKIN (597)		CALLED (592)
	ZEDEKIAH (597-586)		PROPHESIED I (592-589)
589	*SIEGE OF JERUSALEM*		BEREAVED (589)
586	*FALL OF JERUSALEM*		PROPHESIED II (586-585)
	NEBUCHADNEZZAR (605-562)		PROPHESIED III (567)

EXILE

RIVER CHEBAR (TEL AVIV)

EZEKIEL PART 2 & 3

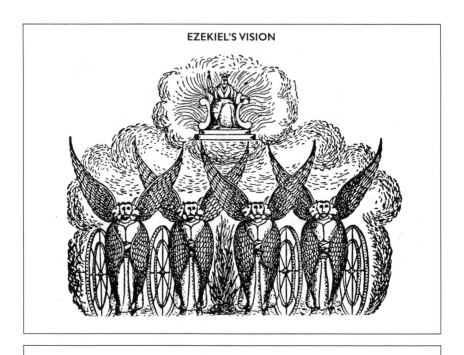

EZEKIEL'S VISION

YEAR OF EXILE	AGE OF EZEKIEL	CONTENT of PROPHECY	CHAPTERS OF BOOK
5th	30	*REDEPLOYMENT of the __PRIEST EZEKIEL__*	1-3
I	5th to 9th	30-33 *	*RETRIBUTION for the CITY JERUSALEM* 'Then y__ou__ will know that I am....' *JERUSALEM BESIEGED (589)*	4-24
II	11th to 12th	36-37	*REVENGE on the NEIGHBOURS of JUDAH* 'Then th__ey__ will know that I am....' *JERUSALEM DESTROYED (587)*	25-32
	12th	37	*RETURN FROM the EXILE in BABYLON* 'Then the __nations__ will know that I am....'	33-39
III	25th	50	*RESTORATION of the __TEMPLE__ in ISRAEL*	40-48

EZEKIEL PART 3

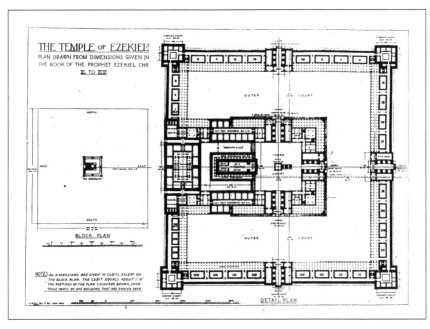

HOLYLAND MODEL (JERUSALEM IN JESUS DAY)

EZEKIEL PART 3

TEMPLE ENTRANCE

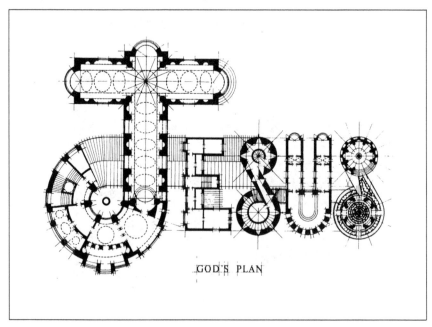

GOD'S PLAN

BABYLON AND BACK

606	*DANIEL*	*First deportation (youth)*
597	*EZEKIEL*	*Second deportation (10,000)*
586	*REST*	*Third deportation (City & Temple destroyed)*
536	*ZERUBBABEL*	*Babylon falls to Persians (539)* *Cyrus allows return (50,000)*
458	*EZRA*	*Temple rebuilt (516)* ESTHER in Susa
445	*NEHEMIAH*	*City walls rebuilt*

NEBUCHADNEZZAR'S DREAM

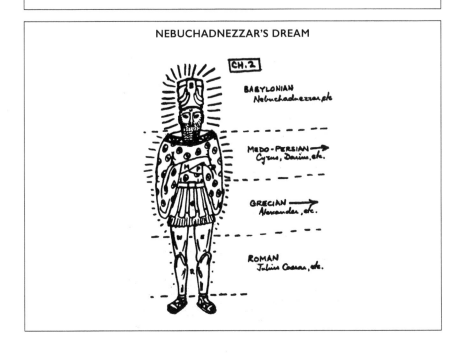

DANIEL PART 1

BABYLON

ISHTAR GATE

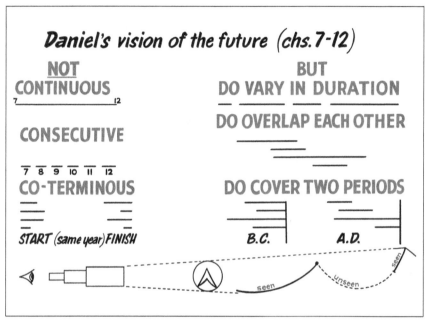

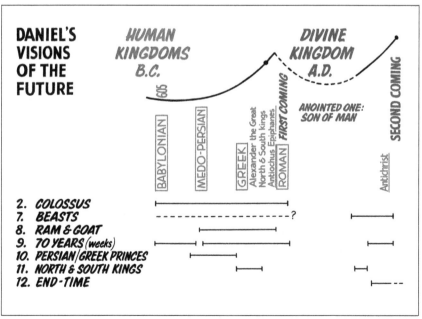

DANIEL PART 2

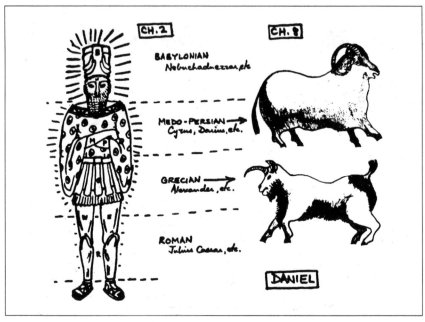

DANIEL PART 2

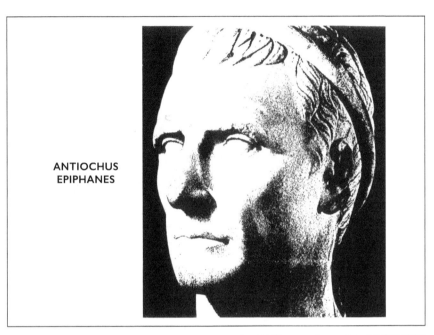

ANTIOCHUS
EPIPHANES

DANIEL PART 2

DANIEL PART 2

NEW WALLS OF BABYLON

HOSEA: A. HUMAN UNFAITHFULNESS

SINS:	SINNERS	SUFFERING
1. INFIDELITY	1. PRIESTS	1. BARRENNESS
2. INDEPENDENCE	2. PROPHETS	2. BLOODSHED
3. INTRIGUE	3. PRINCES	3. BANISHMENT
*4. IDOLATRY	4. PROFITEERS	
5. IGNORANCE		
*6. IMMORALITY		
7. INGRATITUDE		

B. DIVINE FAITHFULNESS

1. GOD CAN'T LET THEM OFF
2. GOD CAN'T LET THEM GO
3. GOD CAN'T LET THEM DOWN

OBADIAH & JOEL

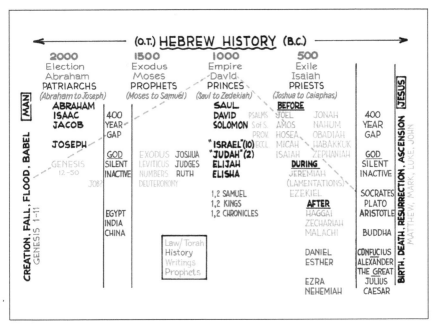

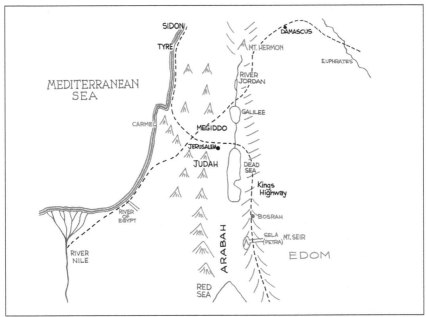

OUTLINE OF OBADIAH

A. ONE NATION JUDGED (1-14)
1. NATIONS DESTROY EDOM (1-9)
2. EDOM DESPISED ISRAEL (10-14)

B. ALL NATIONS JUDGED (15-21)
1. YAHWEH PUNISHES NATIONS (15-16)
2. ISRAEL POSSESSES EDOM (17-21)

PETRA SIQ

OBADIAH & JOEL

PETRA TEMPLE

MT. SEIR (EDOM)

OBADIAH & JOEL

LOCUSTS

OUTLINE OF JOEL

A. PLAGUE OF LOCUSTS (ch.1.)
1. RUIN OF THE LAND (1-12)
2. REPENTANCE OF THE PEOPLE (13-20)

B. DAY OF LORD (ch.2.)
1. TERRIBLE REPETITION (1-11)
2. TRUE REPENTANCE (12-17)
3. TIMELESS RECOVERY (18-27)
4. TOTAL RESTORATION (28-32)
   a. Spirit ~ men and women (28-29)
   b. Signs ~ sun and moon (30-31)
   c. Salvation ~ calling and called (32)

C. VALLEY OF DECISION (ch.3.)
1. VENGEANCE ON NATIONS (1-16a)
2. VINDICATION OF ISRAEL (16b-21)

OBADIAH & JOEL

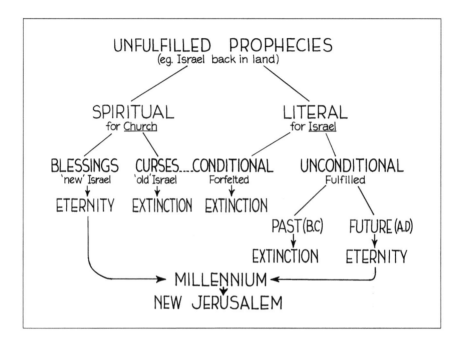

AMOS

"FOR THREE SINS, EVEN FOR FOUR...."

1. INHUMANITY OF ISRAEL'S NEIGHBOURS
DAMASCUS - cruelty
GAZA - brutality
TYRE - treachery

2. INFAMY OF ISRAEL'S COUSINS
EDOM - ruthlessness
AMMON - barbarity
MOAB - sacrilege

3. INFIDELITY OF ISRAEL'S SISTER
JUDAH - rejecting laws of God
accepting lies of men

4. INSENSITIVITY OF ISRAEL'S CHILDREN
ISRAEL - exploiting poor among men
indulging flesh before God

PAST REDEMPTION means FUTURE RETRIBUTION

PROFETS

A. HEAR FROM GOD

WORDS - 'burdens'

PICTURES - visions (awake)
dreams (asleep)

SPIRIT

GOD → MIND → MOUTH

BODY

B. SPEAK FOR GOD

CHALLENGE -
when doing wrong

COMFORT -
when doing right

FALSE - only comfort

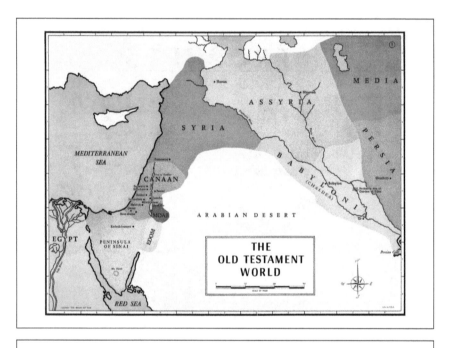

B.C.	ASSYRIA	ISRAEL
1354	AHSURUBALIT I *(First king)*	*(north kings)*
853	SHALMANESER III ——→ *Failed invasion*	AHAB
c.770	←—— JONAH	JEREBOAM II
733	TIGLATH-PILESER III —→ *took Naptali*	PEKAH
721	SHALMANESER V —→*took Israel (10 North tribes)*	HOSHEA *(south kings)*
701	SENNACHERIB —→ *besieged Jerusalem*	HEZEKIAH
663	ASSUR BANIPAL —→ *conquered Thebes (upper Eqypt)*	
c.630	←—— ZEPHANIAH	
c.620	←—— NAHUM	JOSIAH
612	SINSHURISHKUN *(fall of Nineveh)*	
607	ASSURBALIT II *(end of Assyria)*	JEHOIACHIM

MIRACLES in JONAH

1. **WIND → STORM**
2. **LOTS → JONAH**
3. **SEA CALMED**
4. **FISH SWALLOWS**
5. **'FISH' VOMITS**
6. **VINE (OVERNIGHT)**
7. **'WORM' (EATS ROOT)**
8. **SCORCHING WIND**

PHILOSOPHIES [WORLD VIEW]	GOD CREATED THEN	GOD CONTROLS NOW	
ATHEISM	X	X	
DEISM	✓	X	SCIENCE
THEISM	✓	✓	SCRIPTURE

NINEVEH

JONAH

NINEVEH'S REMAINS

JOPPA (JAFFA)

**KIKAYON
(CASTOR OIL
OR RICINUS
PLANT)**

MICAH

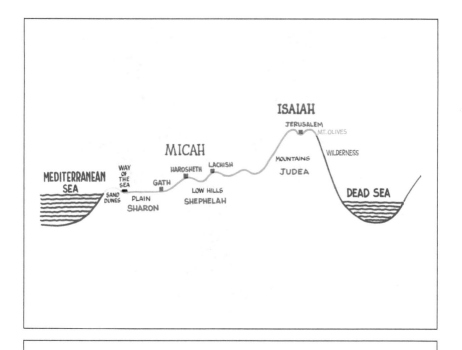

KINGS: JOTHAN: Good, but.   750-731
AHAZ: Bad.   735-715
HEZEKIAH: Very good. 715-686

After Solomon died, civil war.
10 Northern tribes 'ISRAEL'. Capital SAMARIA. Many dynasties.
2 Southern tribes 'JUDAH.' Capital JERUSALEM. One dynasty.

SIN SPREADING
    From north to south. From city to country.

IDOLATRY ~ way people insulted God
IMMORALITY ~ way people indulged themselves
INJUSTICE ~ way people injured each other

MICAH'S VISION: MICAH'S MOTIVATION
    TRIBAL ~ JUDAH   HOLY SPIRIT 3^8
    NATIONAL ~'ISRAEL'   HUMAN SPIRIT 1^8
    UNIVERSAL ~ NATIONS

MICAH
OUTLINE

A. CRIME & PUNISHMENT (1-3)
THE PLACES
THE PEOPLE

B. PEACE & SECURITY (4-5)
THE KINGDOM (after Babylon)
THE KING   (from Bethlehem)

C. JUSTICE & MERCY (6-7)
THE COURT
THE COVENANT

B.C.	ASSYRIA	ISRAEL
1354	AHSURUBALIT I *(First king)*	*(north kings)*
853	SHALMANESER III ⟶ *Failed invasion*	AHAB
c.770	⟵ JONAH	JEREBOAM II
733	TIGLATH-PILESER III ⟶ *took Naptali*	PEKAH
721	SHALMANESER V ⟶ *took Israel (10 North tribes)*	HOSHEA
701	SENNACHERIB ⟶ *besieged Jerusalem*	*(south kings)*
663	ASSUR BANIPAL ⟶ *conquered Thebes (upper Egypt)*	⎱ HEZEKIAH
c.630	⟵ ZEPHANIAH	
c.620	⟵ NAHUM	⎰ JOSIAH
612	SINSHURISHKUN *(fall of Nineveh)*	
607	ASSURBALIT II *(end of Assyria)*	JEHOIACHIM

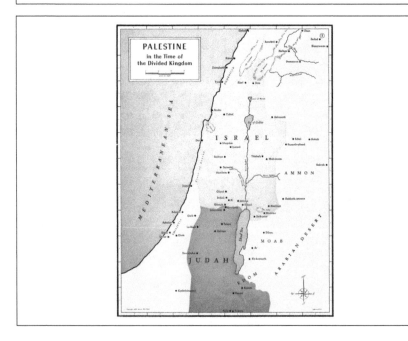

PALESTINE
in the Time of
the Divided Kingdom

NAHUM – *fall of Nineveh*

1. PROCLAMATION [WHO?] INTERVENTION
- *a. DISASTER FOR HIS ENEMIES*
- *b. DELIVERANCE FOR HIS FRIENDS*

2. DESCRIPTION [HOW?] INVASION
- *a. DAY OF LOOTING*
- *b. DEN OF LIONS*

3. EXPLANATION [WHY?] INHUMANITY
- *a. CONQUEST BY FORCE*
- *b. CORRUPTION BY FINANCE*

NINEVEH

NINEVEH'S REMAINS

PROPHETS REVEAL  **YAHWEH 'I AM' ALWAYS**

1. **HIS ACTIVITY -** *POWERFUL*
   NATURE: *MIRACLES*
   HISTORY: *MOVEMENTS*

2. **HIS INTEGRITY -** *PREDICTABLE*
   JUSTICE: *PUNISHMENT*
   MERCY: *PARDON*

3. **HIS FLEXIBILITY -** *PERSONAL*
   MAN: *REPENTS*
   GOD: *RELENTS*

HABAKKUK

Chapters 1-2	Chapter 3
Wrestling with God	Resting in God
Miserable	Happy
Shouting	Singing
Prayer	Praise
Impatient	Patient
Asks for justice	Asks for mercy
Down in dumps!	On a high!

HABAKKUK
THE PROPHET (1¹)
A. COMPLAINING PRAYER (1²-2²⁰)

1. GOD DOES TOO LITTLE (1²⁻¹¹)
   QUESTION: Why don't bad suffer?
   ANSWER: Bad will suffer – Babylonians!

2. GOD DOES TOO MUCH (1¹²-2²⁰)
   QUESTIONS: Why use worse to punish bad?
   Why do good suffer?
   ANSWERS: Good will survive!
   Worse will suffer!

B. COMPOSED PRAISE (3¹⁻¹⁹)

1. TREMBLES AT GOD'S PAST ACTION (1-16)
2. TRUSTS IN GOD'S FUTURE PROTECTION (17-19)

ZEPHANIAH

ZEPHANIAH
THE MESSENGER (1¹)   THE MESSAGE (1²⁻³)
A. FOREIGN RELIGION (1⁴-2³)   B. FOREDOOMED REGION (2⁴⁻¹⁵)

J U D G E M E N T (vertical, left margin)

1. DESERVED (4-6)   1. WEST ～ Philistia (4-7)
2. DECLARED (7-9)   2. EAST ～ Moab, Ammon (8-11)
3. DESCRIBED (10-17)   3. SOUTH ～ Egypt, Ethiopia (12)
4. DEFLECTED (1-3)   4. NORTH ～ Assyria (13-15)

C. FUTURE REDEMPTION (3¹⁻²⁰)

1. CURSE ～ divine justice (1-8)
   a. *NATIONAL OBSTINACY (1-7)*
   i. Rebelling (1-4)   ii. Resisting (5-7)
   b. *INTERNATIONAL OBLITERATION (8)*

2. BLESSING ～ divine mercy (9-20)
   a. *INTERNATIONAL GODLINESS (9)*
   b. *NATIONAL GLADNESS (10-20)*
   i. Rejoicing (10-17)   ii. Returning (18-20)

	ZEPHANIAH	REVELATION
Judgement on God's people	1¹-2³	1-3
Judgements on nations	2⁴⁻¹⁵	4-19
Day of judgement	3¹⁻⁸	20
Final bliss	3⁹⁻²⁰	21-22
	(old Jerusalem)	(new Jerusalem)
	GOD comes as King	JESUS comes again as King

HAGGAI

1. A DEPRESSED PEOPLE (1^1-11) 1/6/2

   YOUR HOUSES ~ DECORATED
   MY HOUSE ~ DEVASTATED

   2. A DETERMINED PEOPLE (1^{12-15}) 24/6/2

      FEARED THE LORD
      OBEYED THE LORD

      3. A DISCOURAGED PEOPLE (2^{1-9}) 21/7/2

         FORMER HOUSE ~ GLORIOUS
         LATTER HOUSE ~ GREATER

4. A DEFILED PEOPLE (2^{10-19}) 24/9/2 | 5. A DESIGNATED PRINCE (2^{20-23}) 24/9/2

   CLEAN DOESN'T MAKE DIRTY CLEAN | OTHER THRONES OVERTURNED
   DIRTY DOES MAKE CLEAN DIRTY | THIS THRONE OCCUPIED

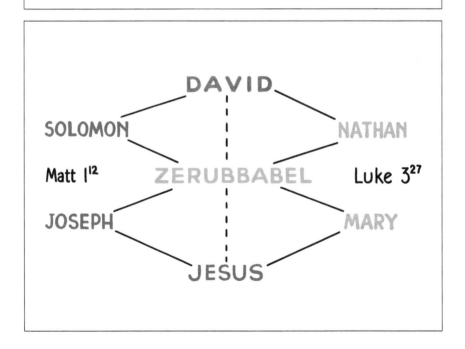

ZECHARIAH

[A] PRESENT PROBLEMS (1-8)

  ① **REBUKE & REBELLION** (1^{1-6}) ?/8/2
      a. ERRING PREDECESSORS   *b.* EARLIER PROPHETS

  ② **ENCOURAGEMENT & ENTHRONEMENT** (1^7-6^{15}) 24/11/2
      a. CRYPTIC PICTURES (1^7-6^8)

    TEMPLE {   i   *FOUR HORSES AMONG MYRTLE TREES*
            ii   *FOUR HORNS AND 'SMITHS'*
    CITY   { iii   *MAN WITH MEASURING LINE*
    LEADERS { iv   *JOSHUA'S CHANGE OF CLOTHES*
             v   *GOLDEN LAMPSTAND & TWO OLIVE TREES*
            { vi   *FLYING SCROLL*
    PEOPLE { vii   *WOMAN IN MEASURING BASKET*
            viii   *FOUR CHARIOTS*

      b. CROWNED PRIEST (6^{9-15})

  ③ **FASTING & FEASTING** (7^1-8^{23}) 4/9/4
      a. SAD REMEMBRANCE (7^{1-14})
      b. GLAD REJOICING (8^{1-23})

[B] FUTURE PREDICTIONS (9-14)

ZECHARIAH

[A] PRESENT PROBLEMS (1-8)   **[B] FUTURE PREDICTIONS** (9-14)

  ① NATIONAL RESTORATION (9-11) (sooner rather than later
      a. VANQUISHED ENEMIES (9^{1-8})
      b. PEACEFUL KING (9^{9-10})
      c. MIGHTY GOD $(9^{11}-10^7)$
      d. GATHERED PEOPLE (10^{8-12})
      e. DEFORESTED NEIGHBOURS (11^{1-3})
      f. WORTHLESS SHEPHERDS (11^{4-17})

  ② INTERNATIONAL REPERCUSSION (12-14) (later rather than soon
      a. INVADING ARMY (12^{1-9})
      b. GRIEVING INHABITANTS (12^{10-14})
      c. BANISHED PROPHETS (13^{1-6})
      d. REDUCED POPULATION (13^{7-9})
      e. PLAGUED ATTACKERS (14^{1-15})
      f. UNIVERSAL WORSHIP (14^{16-25})

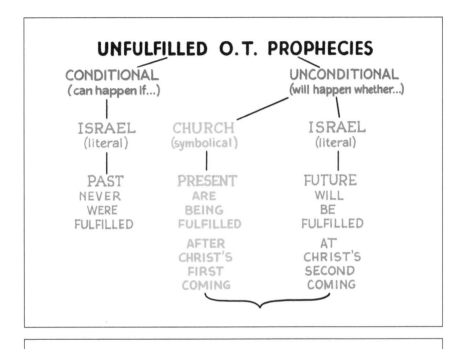

UNFULFILLED O.T. PROPHECIES

CONDITIONAL
(can happen if...)

UNCONDITIONAL
(will happen whether...)

ISRAEL
(literal)

CHURCH
(symbolical)

ISRAEL
(literal)

PAST
NEVER
WERE
FULFILLED

PRESENT
ARE
BEING
FULFILLED

AFTER
CHRIST'S
FIRST
COMING

FUTURE
WILL
BE
FULFILLED

AT
CHRIST'S
SECOND
COMING

MALACHI ⌐ OUTLINE

A. **PAST SURVIVAL** (1¹⁻⁵)
  1. JACOB - ISRAEL - LOVED
  2. ESAU - EDOM - HATED

B. **PRESENT SINS** (1⁶-3¹⁵)
1. PRIESTS (1⁶-2⁹)
  a. *CHEAP SACRIFICES*
  b. *POPULAR SERMONS*

2. PEOPLE (2¹⁰-3¹⁵)
  a. *MIXED MARRIAGES*
  b. *HEARTLESS DIVORCES*
  c. *DOUBTFUL QUESTIONS*
  d. *UNPAID TITHES*
  e. *SLANDEROUS TALK*

C. **FUTURE SEPARATION** (3¹⁶-4⁶)
1. RIGHT CHOICE (3¹⁶-4³)
  a. *RIGHTEOUS*
    Healing in the sun
  b. *WICKED*
    Burning in the fire

2. LAST CHANCE (4⁴⁻⁶)
  a. *MOSES*
    Lawgiver
  b. *ELIJAH*
    Forerunner

NEW
TESTAMENT

FOUR GOSPELS

MARK ~ **SON OF MAN**
MATTHEW ~ **KING OF JEWS**
LUKE ~ **SAVIOUR OF WORLD**
JOHN ~ **SON OF GOD**

THREE STAGES

1. **WHAT JESUS DID** (MARK)
2. **WHAT JESUS SAID** (MATTHEW, LUKE)
3. **WHAT JESUS WAS** (JOHN)

TWO ANGLES

1. **WRITER ~ INSIGHT**
   What?   How?

2. **READER ~ INTENTION**
   Who?   Why?

MARK

a. **BUILDING UP**
   i. 30 months in north (GALILEE)
   ii. 6 months in south (JUDEA)
b. **SLOWING DOWN**
   Years, months, weeks, days, hours.

MATTHEW (using Mark)

a. **SIZE**
   Additions (eg. birth)
   Alterations
   Omissions
b. **SPEECH**
   Sayings · Sermons
c. **STRUCTURE**
   Alternating | words
   (5x) | deeds

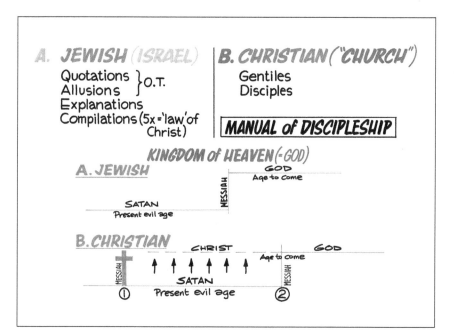

SUBJECTS of the KINGDOM

5-7 LIFESTYLE (Sermon on Mount)
9-10 MISSION
13 GROWTH
18 COMMUNITY
24-25 FUTURE

SONS OF THE FATHER (44x)

Special themes:
FAITH (believing)
RIGHTEOUSNESS (doing)
JUDGEMENT (hell)

MARK

FOUR GOSPELS

MARK ~ **SON OF MAN**
MATTHEW~ **KING OF JEWS**
LUKE ~ **SAVIOUR OF WORLD**
JOHN ~ **SON OF GOD**

THREE STAGES
1. **WHAT JESUS DID** (MARK)
2. **WHAT JESUS SAID** (MATTHEW, LUKE)
3. **WHAT JESUS WAS** (JOHN)

TWO ANGLES
1. **WRITER ~ INSIGHT**
   What?   How?
2. **READER ~ INTENTION**
   Who?   Why?

FOUR GOSPELS

WRITERS: a. DEVELOPING INTEREST
What he did (Mark)
What he said (Luke, Matthew)
What he was (John)

b. DIFFERING INSIGHT
King of Jews (Matthew)
Son of man (Mark)
Saviour of world (Luke)
Son of God (John)

READERS: a. BELIEVERS
Matthew (younger)
John (older)

b. UNBELIEVERS
Mark
Luke

MARK

| CAESAREA PHILIPPI | GETHSEMANE |

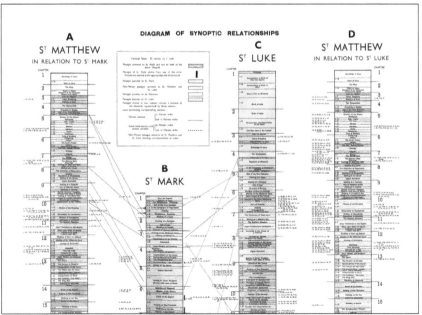

Larger version available from: www.davidpawson.com/synopticrelationshipdiagram

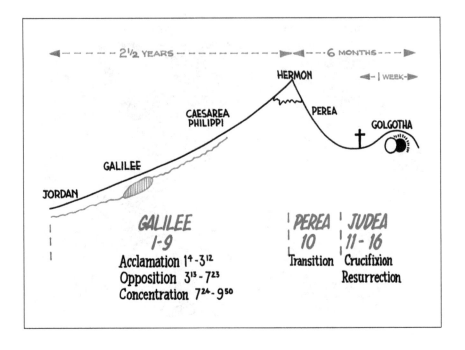

SAMARITAN'S INN

ROAD TO EMMAUS

PRODIGAL SON? (15$^{11\text{-}23}$)
PRODIGAL FATHER! (15-16)
(WITH TWO LOST SONS)

15$^{1\text{-}2}$	15$^{3\text{-}10}$	15$^{11\text{-}32}$	16$^{1\text{-}31}$
TAX COLLECTORS SINNERS (1) Eating inside	LOST SHEEP (3-7) Lost far away Knew it	YOUNGER SON (13-23) 'wasted'	ROGUE (1-9) 'wasted'
PHARISEES SCRIBES (2) Murmuring outside	LOST COIN (8-10) Lost at home Didn't know it	ELDER SON (24-32) 'righteous'	RICH MAN (15-31) 'righteous

Who is the 'father'?
Which 'son' is the story about?
How did it end?

LUKE

Larger version available from: www.davidpawson.com/synopticrelationshipdiagram

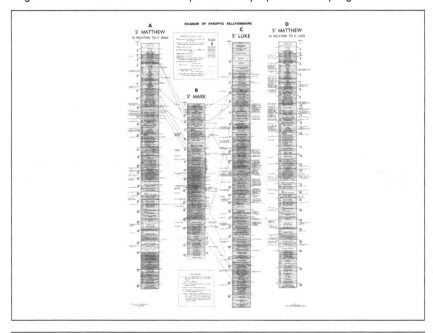

UNIQUE MATERIAL	PEOPLE INTEREST	SUPERNATURAL DIMENSION
BIRTH	SAMARITANS	ANGELS
BOYHOOD	GENTILES	PRAYER
GENEALOGY	OUTCASTS	HOLY SPIRIT
TEACHING	WOMEN	WORSHIP
PARABLES	'POOR'	FUTURE
INCIDENTS	'SINNERS'	
ASCENSION		

JOHN ~contrast to 'Synoptics'

1. **OMISSIONS**
2. **ADDITIONS**
3. **EMPHASIS**   M →
4. **STYLE**   M →
5. **OUTLOOK**   L →

SYNOPTICS - TIME (horizontal) <u>Hebrew</u>
    Present: future. "age"
JOHN - SPACE (vertical) <u>Greek</u>
    Below: above. "world"

A. **THE PERSON** (who wrote it)
    The disciple who loved.
    The apostle who lived.
B. **THE PURPOSE** (for which he wrote.)
    End ~ LIFE (have) noun
    Means ~ BELIEVE (do) verb

BELIEVING (98x)
    1. **CREDENCE** ~ believing THAT
        Accepting the truth (words and works.)
    2. **CONFIDENCE** ~ believing IN
        Doing the truth (trust and obey.)
    3. **CONTINUANCE** ~ GO ON believing
        Holding the truth (faith & faithfulness)

TRUTH ~ not a proposition
        but a person.

    a. **TOO HIGH A VIEW OF JOHN**
    b. **TOO LOW A VIEW OF JESUS**
            More divine than human?
            More human than divine?
            Partly human, partly divine?
            <u>Fully</u> human, <u>fully</u> divine!

THE TRUTH ABOUT JESUS IS THE TRUTH.

HIS FULL HUMANITY
HIS FULL DIVINITY

SEVEN WITNESSES	SEVEN WORKS	SEVEN WORDS
John the B.	Water into wine	Bread of heaven
Nathaniel	Nobleman's son	Light of world
Jesus	Bethesda cripple	Good shepherd
Peter	Feeding 5000	"I AM" Door of fold
Martha	Walking on water	Resurrection & life
Thomas	Blind man	Way, truth, life
John	Lazarus	True vine

GLORY ～ only begotten Son
           the Father

LOGOS ～ the word?
           the reason why!
a. His ETERNITY
b. His PERSONALITY
c. His DEITY
d. His HUMANITY

LIFE   Life/death
            Light / darkness
            Truth / lies
            freedom/Slavery
            Love / wrath

To know the Father
To know the Son

JOHN PART 2

HOLY SPIRIT

Ch. 1.	Baptised with Baptiser 'in'
Ch. 3.	Born again Born 'out of'
Ch. 4.	Living water True worship
Ch. 7.	Feast of tabernacles Springs of water
Chs. 14-16	Paraclete - called beside. Encourager, standby. Spirit of truth 'Another' comforter.
Ch. 20.	Sign : blew Command: receive!

LUKE ~ doctor · Gentile · traveller
            writer · evangelist
THEOPHILUS ~ representative?
(Mr. Godfriendly)   individual?

A. HISTORICAL

1. Two Sections: **Peter to Jews** (1-12)
                  Paul to Gentiles (13-28)

2. Three Sections: **Jerusalem** (1-7)
                    Judea & Samaria (8-10)
                    Ends of the earth (11-28)

3. Five Sections: **Jews - Jerusalem** _____ 6.7
                   Hellenists & Samaritans _____ 9.31
                   Gentiles - Antioch _____ 12.24
                   Asia _____ 16.5
                   Europe _____ 19.20
                   Rome

B. EXISTENTIAL

1. *LINK* ~ **BETWEEN GOSPELS & EPISTLES.**
            PAUL
            BAPTISM IN WATER
            BAPTISM IN SPIRIT
            LAW OF MOSES
            CHURCH

2. *MODEL* ~ **MISSIONARY MANUAL**
            BAD AS WELL AS GOOD
            ABNORMAL AS WELL AS NORMAL

            SEND APOSTLES
            REACH CITIES
            PREACH GOSPEL
            MAKE DISCIPLES
            PLANT CHURCHES
            APPOINT ELDERS - MOVE ON!

Roland Allen
(December 29, 1868
– June 9, 1947)

C. TRINITARIAN

TITLE: "ACTS" OF APOSTLES?
JESUS?
HOLY SPIRIT?
<u>GOD!</u>

CONTENTS: **THE KINGDOM OF GOD** (The Father)
THE NAME OF JESUS (The Son)
THE POWER OF THE HOLY SPIRIT

WRITER ~ PAUL
STATEMENT
ARGUMENT
WRITER & READERS ~ PAUL & ROME
CAPITAL OF THE EMPIRE
GATEWAY TO THE WEST
READERS ~ ROME
EXTERNAL ~ CITY (Political & Social)
INTERNAL ~ CHURCH
(i) Jewish   (ii) Gentile   (iii) Gentile & Jewish

KEY WORDS: GOD (153x)
LAW (72x)
CHRIST (65x)
SIN (48x)
LORD (43x)
FAITH (40x)

KEY CONCEPT: RIGHTEOUSNESS
v. GENTILE UNRIGHTEOUSNESS
v. JEWISH RIGHTEOUSNESS
1. *IMPUTED - JUSTIFICATION (Penalty of sin)*
2. *IMPARTED - SANCTIFICATION (Power of sin)*
3. *COMPLETED - GLORIFICATION (Presence of sin)*

SALVATION

OUTLINE: *FAITH (1-4)   HOPE (5-11)   LOVE (12-16)*

HIS MESSAGE (GOD, SON, SPIRIT)   1.
CORPORATE GREETINGS   1.

1. **PAUL'S ACCOUNT of HIS GOSPEL (1-8)**
   a. RIGHTEOUSNESS REVEALED IN <u>GOD'S</u> WRATH.   1-3
   b. RIGHTEOUSNESS CREDITED THROUGH <u>CHRIST'S</u> DEATH.   3-5
   c. RIGHTEOUSNESS ACHIEVED BY <u>SPIRIT'S</u> LIFE.   6-8

2. **PAUL'S AGONY OVER HIS PEOPLE (9-11)**
   a. ISRAEL'S <u>PAST</u> REDUCTION TO THE REMNANT.   9
   b. ISRAEL'S <u>PRESENT</u> RESISTANCE TO THE GOSPEL.   10
   c. ISRAEL'S <u>FUTURE</u> RESTORATION TO THE COVENANT.   11

3. **PAUL'S APPEAL TO HIS READERS (12-16)**
   a. THEIR PERSONAL BEARING IN SERVICE & SUFFERING.   12
   b. THEIR PUBLIC BEHAVIOUR IN STATE & SOCIETY.   13
   c. THEIR PRACTICAL BROTHERHOOD IN SCRUPLES & SONG.   14-15

HIS METHOD (WORD, DEED & SIGN).   15
INDIVIDUAL GREETINGS.   16

1 & 2 CORINTHIANS PART 1

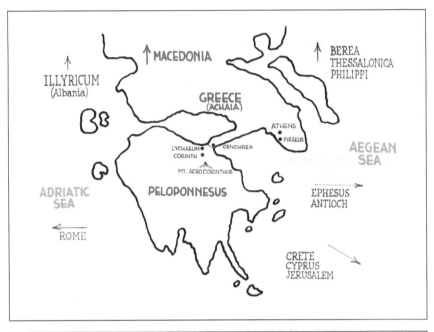

CORINTH

CANAL

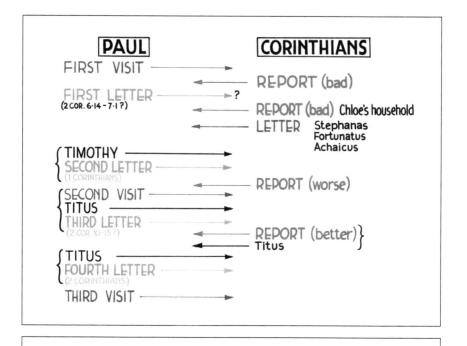

I. CORINTHIANS

FORGETTING CRUCIFIXION

REPORTS   REQUESTS

DIVISION
IMMORALITY
LITIGATION
         MARRIAGE/DIVORCE
IDOLATRY
MEN / WOMEN
       MEAT
LORD'S SUPPER
       SPIRITUAL GIFTS

DOUBTING RESURRECTION
FAMINE RELIEF

LOVE

TO LUST	TO LIKE	TO LOVE
EROS	PHILADELPHIA	AGAPE
EPITHUMEA		
ATTRACTION	AFFECTION	ATTENTION
BODY	MIND	WILL
EMOTIONAL	INTELLECTUAL	VOLITIONAL
DEPENDENT	INTERDEPENDENT	INDEPENDENT

MARRIAGE

SEXUAL	SOCIAL	SACRIFICIAL

2. CORINTHIANS

1-7 DEFENCE OF HIMSELF
Tender appeal
Sincerity

8-9 FAMINE RELIEF

10-13 ATTACK ON OTHERS
Tough accusation
Sarcasm

WRITER: *PAUL (the apostle)*

READERS: *CHURCHES in GALATIA (north or south?)*

OCCASION: *1. ADDITIONS to the MESSAGE*
2. ATTACKS on the MESSENGER

ISSUE: *a. CIRCUMCISION?*
b. JUDAISM?
c. SALVATION!
    i. WORKS ALONE.
    ii. WORKS PLUS FAITH.
    iii. FAITH PLUS WORKS.
    iv. FAITH ALONE.

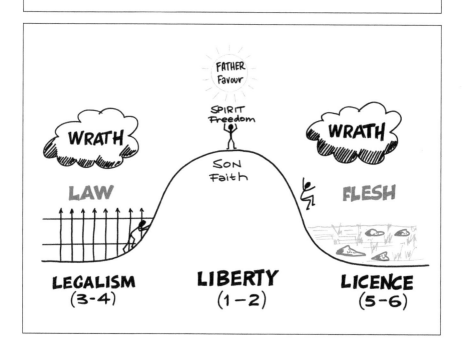

STRIDING EDGE, LAKE DISTRICT, UK

EPHESIANS

EPHESUS

EPHESIANS

CHAPTERS 1-3	CHAPTERS 4-6
RELATIONSHIP TO GOD (IN CHRIST)	RELATIONSHIP TO OTHERS (IN THE LORD)
SALVATION WORKED IN DOCTRINE	SALVATION WORKED OUT DUTY
WHAT WE ARE SAVED BY FORGIVENESS	WHAT WE ARE SAVED FOR HOLINESS
JUSTIFICATION	SANCTIFICATION
OUR RELEASE	OUR RESPONSE
ADORATION	APPLICATION
DIVINE SOVEREIGNTY	HUMAN RESPONSIBILITY
HIS | PURPOSE	OUR | WALK
| POWER	| WARFARE
Inside 'church' Vertical dimension	Outside 'church' Horizontal dimension

EPHESIANS 1-3

PRAISING (1. 3-14)
GOD'S PURPOSE to sum up all things in Christ
PRAYING (1. 15-17)
GOD'S PURPOSE AND POWER to know
PREACHING (1. 19-3.13)
GOD'S POWER AND PURPOSE revealed in:
> 1. CHRIST (1. 20-23)
>   *RAISED UP TO REIGN*
> 2. GENTILES (2. 1-22)
>   *RAISED UP TO REJOIN*
> 3. PAUL (3. 1-13)
>   *RAISED UP TO REVEAL*

PRAYING (3. 14-19)
GOD'S POWER AND PURPOSE to know.
PRAISING (3. 20)
GOD'S POWER to do exceeding abundantly.

EPHESIANS

TEMPLE MIDDLE WALL PARTITION

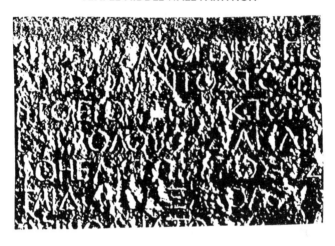

"WHOEVER IS CAUGHT DOING SO WILL HAVE
HIMSELF TO BLAME IF DEATH ENSUES."

EPHESIANS 4-6

A. OUR WALK (4.1 -6.9)
    1. HUMILITY
    2. UNITY
    3. MATURITY
    4. INTEGRITY
    5. CHARITY
    6. PURITY
    7. DOCILITY   a. Wives
                       b. Children
                       c. Slaves (employees)
    8. RESPONSIBILITY   a. Husbands
                               b. Parents
                               c. Masters (employers)

B. OUR WARFARE (6.10-20)
    1. PROTECTION
    2. PRAYER

EPHESIANS

PREDESTINATION

TO SALVATION	TO SERVICE
INDIVIDUAL PERSONS	CORPORATE A PEOPLE
IRRESISTIBLE GRACE	CONDITIONAL FAITH
Destiny determined (by God's choice).	Destiny dependent (on our choice).
Lost because not chosen.	Lost because wrong choice.
Born again before repenting and believing.	Born again after repenting and believing.
Perseverance guaranteed.	Perseverance required.

THOSE WHO PERSEVERE

CALVIN will be saved ARMINIUS

are predestined to glory

PHILIPPIANS & PHILEMON PART I

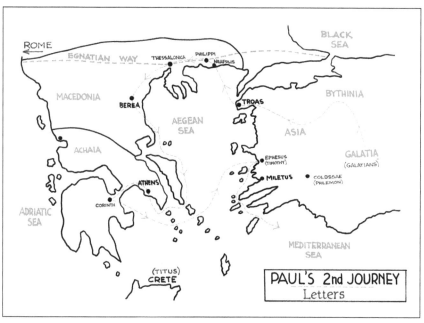

PHILIPPI

PHILIPPIANS & PHILEMON PART I & 2

Paul Robert Schneider
(August 29, 1897 – July 18, 1939)

The first protestant minister
to be martyred by the Nazis.

PHILIPPIANS 3.

1. REDEMPTION ~ an experience to apply
    a. God works it in
    b. We work it out

2. RIGHTEOUSNESS ~ an end to pursue
    a. Not ours: birth and life
    b. But his: death and resurrection

3. RESPONSIBILITY ~ an effort to make
    a. Forgetting about the past
    b. Forging ahead to the future

4. REPRODUCTION ~ an example to follow
    a. Bad: earthly minded
    b. Good: heavenly minded

5. RESURRECTION ~ an event to desire
    a. Out from the dead
    b. With a new body

ANCIENT LETTERS

1. PERSONAL ~ individual (Philemon)
2. OCCASIONAL ~ local (Colossians)
3. GENERAL ~ encyclical (Ephesians)

Read between lines: circumstances
situation
crisis
need

WHAT does he <u>correspond</u> to?
WHO does he <u>correspond</u> with?
WHY does he <u>correspond</u> at all?

Pattern: SENDER
RECEIVER (address)
GREETING (prayers/wishes)
COMPLIMENT (or thanks)
SUBSTANCE (one or more topics)
SUMMARY
GREETING

Biblical 'epistles': REALITY (past): actual practice
RELEVANCE (present): applied principle

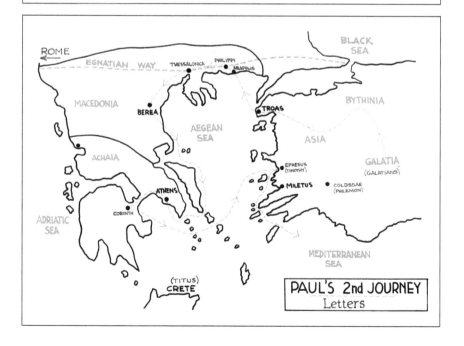

PAUL'S 2nd JOURNEY
Letters

© David Pawson 2017

COLOSSIANS

**ROAD TO
COLOSSAE
(MEANDERING
RIVER)**

COLOSSIANS

A. SYNCRETISM: religion of Christianity

1. REDUCED BELIEF
a. Immanence of God (too high)
b. Pre-eminence of Christ (too low)

2. REGULATED BEHAVIOUR
a. Observance of calendar
b. Abstinence of body

B. SIMPLICITY: relation to Christ

1. ALL DIVINE FULNESS IN THE ETERNAL CHRIST
a. CREATOR of the universe.
b. CONQUEROR of the powers.
c. CONTROLLER of the church.

2. ALL HUMAN FOCUS ON THE EXALTED CHRIST
a. PURITY in the passions.
b. CHARITY in the church.
c. HARMONY in the home.
  i. Wives/husbands.
  ii. Children/parents.
  iii. Slaves/masters.

1 & 2 THESSALONIANS PART 1 & 2

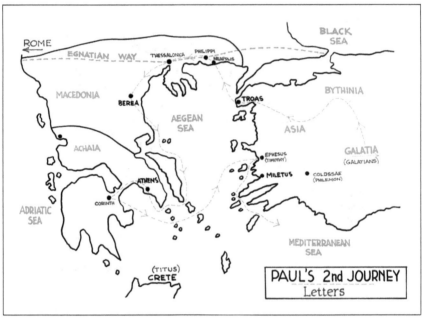

I (WARM)   **THESSALONIANS**   II (COOL)

We pray for you

A. THEIR RECEPTIVITY (1)
1. Word, deed and sign
2. Faith, hope and love
3. God, Jesus, Spirit
4. Turn, serve, wait

B. HIS INTEGRITY (2-3)
1. Flatters when present
2. Forgets when absent

C. THEIR MATURITY (4-5)
1. HOLINESS
    Women. Work.
2. HOPE
    Dead. Date.
LEADERS, MEMBERS,
SPIRIT, GOD, JESUS
You pray for us

A. THEIR TENACITY (1)
1. Human injustice in present
2. Divine justice in future

We pray for you

B. THEIR STABILITY (2-3)
1. HOPE
    Date. Delay.
You pray for us
2. HOLINESS
    Work

1 & 2 THESSALONIANS PART 2

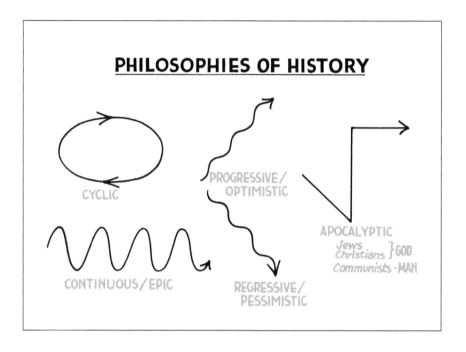

I, 2 TIMOTHY, TITUS

UNLIKE THE OTHERS
LIKE EACH OTHER
AUTHORSHIP?   STYLE
              CONTENT
              ITINERARY

Paul older, facing death
Churches older, facing death

"PASTORAL"?   Manual for pastors
              Internal rather than external

"EVANGELISTIC"?   Character of churches
                  Influence of churches

"APOSTOLIC"!   Pioneering
               Temporary

Three ways to study: WRITER (Paul)
                       READERS (Titus & Timothy)
                       ADDRESS (Crete & Ephesus)

PAUL   A. PATTERN OF HIS LIFE
        1. Past changes
        2. Present circumstances
        3. Future prospects

        B. PURPOSE OF HIS LIFE
           1. OBJECTIVE ~ divine indicative
              a. GOD ~ saviour and king
              b. JESUS ~ saviour and judge
              c. HOLY SPIRIT ~ gift and gifts
           2. SUBJECTIVE ~ human imperative
              a. EXPERIENTIAL ~ past justification
              b. ETHICAL ~ present sanctification
              c. ESCHATOLOGICAL ~ future glorification

TITUS   TOUGH GENTILE (uncircumcised)
TIMOTHY   TIMID JEW (circumcised)

GOSPEL: SALVATION

A. OBJECTIVE ~ DIVINE (indicative)
1. GOD   Only, immortal, invisible, living, etc.
2. CHRIST JESUS   Birth, death, resurrection, ascension, return
3. HOLY SPIRIT   Gift experienced, gifts exercised

B. SUBJECTIVE ~ HUMAN (imperative)
1. JUSTIFICATION ~ PAST: PENALTY (experiential)
    Water baptism
    Spirit baptism
2. SANCTIFICATION ~ PRESENT: POWER (ethical)
    Separated from evil
    Set apart for good
3. GLORIFICATION ~ FUTURE: PRESENCE (eschatological)
    Need for perseverance
    Reward for perseverance

	TITUS (CRETE)	**TIMOTHY** (EPHESUS)
ELDERS	None	Wrong
CONCERN	Membership	Leadership
ERROR	Peripheral	Central

1. TO COMPLETE THE TRANSITION
    a. *Quality leaders*
    b. *Quality members*

2. TO CONFRONT THE TROUBLERS
    a. *Errors they propagated*
    b. *Example they presented*
    c. *Effect they produced*

3. TO COMMUNICATE THE TRUTH
    a. *Message to be declared*
    b. *Model to be demonstrated*

"EXHORTATION" ~ *NEGATIVE: DON'T GO BACK!*
(APPEAL) *POSITIVE: DO GO ON!*
"Let us..." (13x, 8x in chs. 11-13)

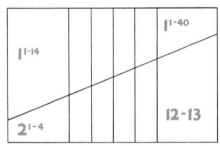

EXPOSITION 1^{1-14} 1^{1-40}

2^{1-4} 12-13 *EXHORTATION*

A. NEGATIVE CONTRAST (1-10) *"DON'T GO BACK"*
1. SON TO SERVANTS (1-6)
BETTER THAN *PROPHETS · ANGELS*
APOSTLES (Moses and Joshua)
PRIESTS (Aaron and sons)
2. SUBSTANCE TO SHADOWS (7-10)
BETTER THAN *PRIESTHOOD (Melchizedek)*
COVENANT (new)
SACRIFICES (once-for-all)
B. POSITIVE CONTINUITY (11-13) *"DO GO ON"*
1. FAITH IN GOD
ABEL · ENOCH · NOAH · ABRAHAM · ISAAC · JACOB · MOSES
JOSEPH · JOSHUA · RAHAB · GIDEON · BARAK · SAMSON
JEPHTHAH · DAVID · SAMUEL and the PROPHETS
2. FOCUS ON JESUS
PIONEER & PERFECTOR of FAITH
MEDIATOR of a NEW COVENANT · SUFFERER OUTSIDE the CAMP.

CONCLUSIONS:

1. POSSIBLE TO LOSE SALVATION.
2. ONCE LOST, IMPOSSIBLE TO RECOVER.
3. PREDESTINATION REQUIRES CONTINUED CO-OPERATION.
4. HOLINESS IS AS NECESSARY AS FORGIVENESS.
5. GOD IS A HOLY GOD.

VALUE:

1. BIBLE STUDY.
2. CHRIST-CENTERED.
3. FAITH-BUILDING.
4. BACK-SLIDING.
5. CHURCH MEMBERSHIP.

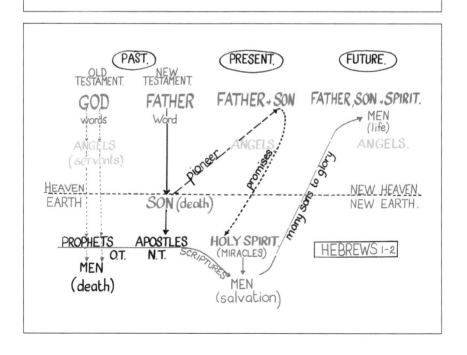

HEBREWS PART 2

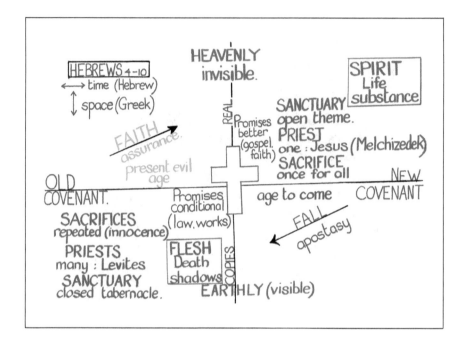

IMPRESSIONS ~ how <u>practical</u>!
how <u>illogical</u>!

WRITER ~ half-brother of Jesus.
presiding elder in Jerusalem.
"the Just" pillar of the church.

STYLE ~ Greek rhetoric.
Hebrew wisdom.

READERS ~ Jewish believers (in DIASPORA)
  i. At home - majority - segregation
     Too strict → PRIDE
  ii. Abroad - minority - assimilation
     Too lax → GREED

CONTENT:
WEALTH *(godlessness)*
WORDS *(blessing & cursing)*
WORLD *(tests & temptations)*
WISDOM *(above & below)*

PROBLEM:
DEEDS RATHER THAN DOCTRINE.
LAW   "   "   GOSPEL.
WORKS   "   "   FAITH.

But "<u>WORKS</u>" = **ACTIONS**

A. SALVATION

1. *INDIVIDUAL* ~ *the word of God*
   A living hope · A tested faith · A joyful love
2. *CORPORATE* ~ *the people of God*
   A spiritual house · A royal priesthood · A holy nation

B. SUFFERING

1. *NOT DESERVED* Right, not wrong
2. *NOT REVENGED* Good, not evil
3. *NOT SUCCESSFUL* Spirit, not body

C. SUBMISSION

1. *SUBJECTS* To rulers (national and local)
2. *SLAVES* To masters (even harsh)
3. *WIVES* To husbands (especially unbelievers)
4. *YOUNGER* To elders (who serve, not lord)

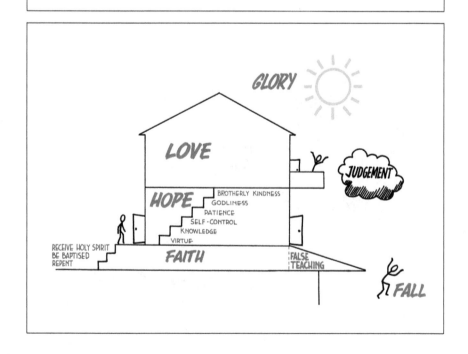

PAUL AND HIS LETTERS

ROAD TO DAMASCUS **STRAIGHT STREET**

ANTIOCH

PAUL AND HIS LETTERS

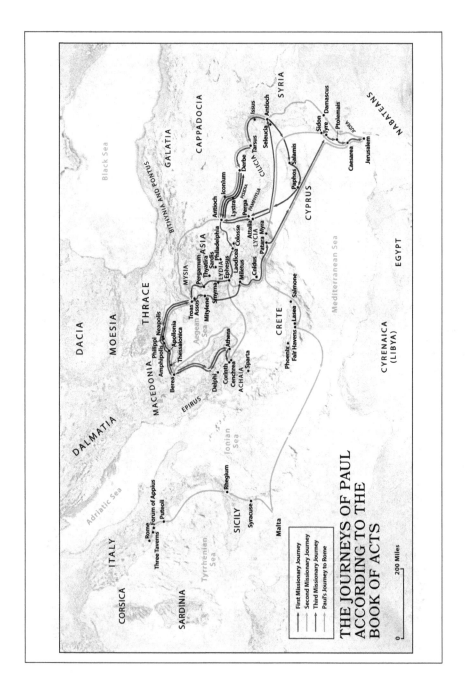

THE JOURNEYS OF PAUL
ACCORDING TO THE
BOOK OF ACTS

First Missionary Journey
Second Missionary Journey
Third Missionary Journey
Paul's Journey to Rome

0   200 Miles

LETTERS OF JOHN PART I

ABSOLUTE CONTRASTS

LIFE	DEATH
LIGHT	DARKNESS
TRUTH	LIES
LOVE	HATE
RIGHTEOUSNESS	LAWLESSNESS
CHILDREN OF GOD	CHILDREN OF SATAN
LOVE OF THE FATHER	LOVE OF THE WORLD

WHO? (2. 12-14)

`LITTLE CHILDREN'	`YOUNG MEN'	`FATHERS'
Know forgiveness	Developed strength	Length of experience
Know fatherhood	Digested scripture	Depth of experience
	Defeated Satan	

WHY?

That they may be **SATISFIED (1.4)**   To promote **HARMONY** (1.3)
SINLESS (2.1)   To produce **HAPPINESS** (1.4)
SAFE (2.26)   To protect **HOLINESS** (2.1)
SURE (5.13)   To prevent **HERESY** (2.26)
     To provide **HOPE** (5.13)

THE WORD

LIFE
LOVE
LIGHT
CHILDREN OF GOD
CHILDREN OF DEVIL
LAWLESSNESS
LUST
LIES

THE WORLD

SANDWICH ⌐ 　positive 　DO
　　　　　　　negative 　DON'T
　　　　　　　positive 　DO

LIFE (1. 1-4)
LIGHT (1.5 - 2.11)
　　　LUST
　　　LIES 　　　　　　　　} (2.15 - 3.10)
　　　LAWLESSNESS
LOVE (3.11 - 4.21)
LIFE (5. 1-21)

FATHER

GOD IS LIGHT
GOD IS LOVE
GOD IS LIFE

CHILDREN

EMBRACE LIGHT
EXPRESS LOVE
ENJOY LIFE

TESTS OF 'TRUE' CHRISTIANS

1. DOCTRINAL: PERSON OF CHRIST
   HERESY

2. SPIRITUAL: RECEPTION OF SPIRIT
   DEVIL

3. MORAL: PRACTICE OF RIGHTEOUSNESS
   LAWLESSNESS

4. SOCIAL: LOVE OF BRETHREN
   HATRED

ASSURANCE ⟶ CONFIDENCE

WITHIN OURSELVES
BEFORE OTHERS
TOWARDS GOD

SIN IN BELIEVERS (3.9)

Is it:

INDUBITABLE ～ we do sin?
INEVITABLE ～ we will sin?
INCOMPATIBLE ～ we should not sin?
INTOLERABLE ～ we must not sin?
INEXCUSABLE ～ we need not sin?
INAPPLICABLE ～ we do not sin?
INCONCEIVABLE ～ we cannot sin?

i. Means exactly what it says.
ii. 'Sin' only means blatant vices and crimes.
iii. God doesn't call it 'sin' in believers.
iv. Refers to our new nature, not old.
v. This is the 'ideal', not the actual.
vi. Only refers to habitual, persistent sin.

Applies to those who are:

BORN of GOD (have his seed/sperm in them)
ABIDING in CHRIST

Not discussing security of believers (5.16) but sinfulness in believers.

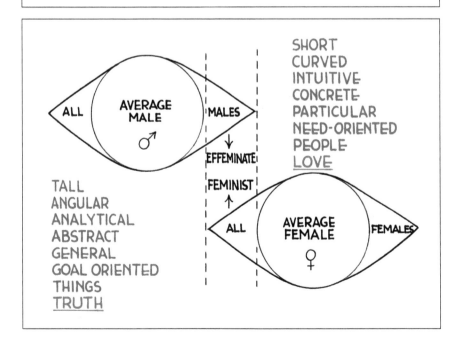

II and III JOHN
HOSPITALITY ~ TRUTH AND LOVE

TO A LADY	TO A MAN
DANGER ~	DANGER ~
TOO MUCH LOVE	TOO MUCH TRUTH
ATTITUDE ~	ATTITUDE ~
TOO SOFT-HEARTED	TOO HARD-HEARTED
DOOR OPEN TOO WIDE	DOOR SHUT TOO TIGHTLY
WELCOME WRONG PEOPLE	REFUSE RIGHT PEOPLE
NEGLECT TRUTH	NEGLECT LOVE
WRONG BELIEF	WRONG BEHAVIOUR
NEED	*BOTH*
Love __and truth__ in woman	*Truth __and love__ in men*

II JOHN   III JOHN

1-3. LOVE IN TRUTH	1. LOVE IN TRUTH
4. FOLLOWING TRUTH	2-4. FOLLOWING TRUTH
5-6. FOLLOWING LOVE	5-8. FOLLOWING LOVE
7-9. SOME REJECT TRUTH	9-10. SOME REFUSE LOVE
10-11. DON'T INVITE THEM	11-12. DON'T IMITATE THEM
12-13. OUR JOY	13-15. YOUR PEACE

JUDE
'CANCER IN THE BODY'

1-16: DANGEROUS CORRUPTION
17-25: DELICATE CORRECTION

1. CREED   a. SENTIMENTAL GOD
              b. SYNCRETISED JESUS

2. CONDUCT   a. ISRAEL IN WILDERNESS
               b. ANGELS AT HERMON
               c. SODOM AND GOMORRAH

3. CHARACTER   a. CAIN – ANGER
                b. BALAAM – AVARICE
                c. KORAH – AMBITION

4. CONVERSATION   a. GRUMBLERS AND FAULT FINDERS
                     b. BOASTERS AND FLATTERERS

1-16: DANGEROUS CORRUPTION
17-25: DELICATE CORRECTION

1. SHOULD HAVE EXPECTED THIS
     a. OLD TESTAMENT PROPHETS
     b. NEW TESTAMENT APOSTLES

2. WILL HAVE TO DEAL WITH THIS
     a. **YOURSELVES**
          BUILD UP IN FAITH
          KEEP IN DIVINE LOVE
          WAIT FOR MERCY IN <u>HOPE</u>
     b. **OTHERS**
          MENTAL DOUBT
          MORTAL DANGER
          MORAL DEFILEMENT

HIS ABILITY – to keep and present
HIS AUTHORITY – only God, our Saviour

REVELATION TALK I

MONASTERY OF SAINT JOHN, PATMOS

REVELATION TALK 2

COVENTRY CATHEDRAL TAPESTRY

GREECE AND TURKEY FROM SPACE

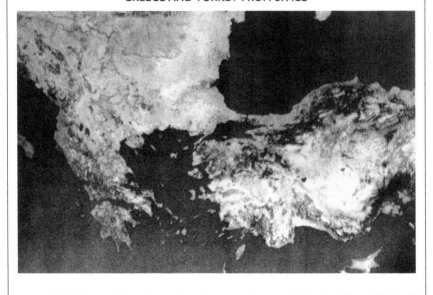

REVELATION TALK 2

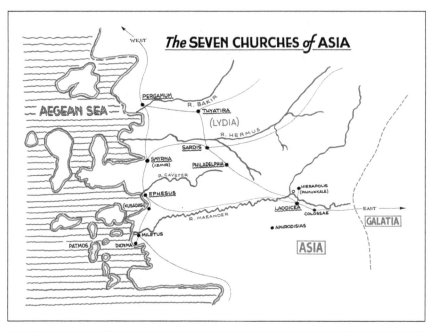

The SEVEN CHURCHES of ASIA

SATAN'S THRONE FROM PERGAMUM (NOW IN BERLIN)

REVELATION TALK 2

1. **ADDRESS**
   "TO THE ANGEL IN...."
2. **ATTRIBUTE**
   "THESE ARE THE WORDS OF HIM WHO...."
3. **APPROVAL**
   "I KNOW YOUR DEEDS...."
4. **ACCUSATION**
   "YET I HOLD THIS AGAINST YOU...."
5. **ADVICE**
   "....OR I WILL COME"
6. **APPEAL**
   "HE WHO HAS AN EAR,
   LET HIM HEAR WHAT
   THE SPIRIT SAYS TO THE CHURCHES"
7. **ASSURANCE**
   "TO HIM WHO OVERCOMES, I WILL....

**EPHESUS
(MAIN STREET)**

REVELATION TALK 2

DIVISION	REF	EPHESUS	REF	SMYRNA	REF	PERGAMUM
ADDRESS	2:1	To the angel of the church in Ephesus write:	2:8	To the angel of the church in Smyrna write:	2:12	To the angel of the church in Pergamum write:
ATTRIBUTE	2:1	These are the words of him who holds the seven stars in his right hand and walks among the seven golden lampstands.	2:8	These are the words of him who is the First and the Last, who died and came to life again.	2:12	These are the words of him who has the sharp, double-edged sword.
APPROVAL	2:2 / 3	I know your deeds, your hard work and your perseverance. I know that you cannot tolerate wicked men, that you have tested those who claim to be apostles but are not, and have found them false. You have persevered and have endured hardships for my name, and have not grown weary.	2:9 / 10	I know your afflictions and your poverty - yet you are rich! I know about the slander of those who say they are Jews and are not, but are a synagogue of Satan. Do not be afraid of what you are about to suffer. I tell you, the devil will put some of you in prison to test you, and you will suffer persecution for ten days.	2:13	I know where you live - where Satan has his throne. Yet you remain true to my name. You did not renounce your faith in me, even in the days of Antipas, my faithful witness, who was put to death in your city - where Satan lives.
ACCUSATION	2:4	Yet I hold this against you: You have forsaken your first love.			2:14 / 15	Nevertheless, I have a few things against you: You have people there who hold to the teaching of Balaam, who taught Balak to entice the Israelites to sin by eating the food sacrificed to idols and committing sexual immorality. Likewise, you also have those who hold to the teaching of the Nicolaitans.
ADVICE	2:5 / 6	Remember the height from which you have fallen! Repent and do the things you did at first. If you do not repent, I will come to you and remove your lampstand from its place. But you have this in your favour: You hate the practices of the Nicolaitans, which I also hate.	2:10	Be faithful, even to the point of death, and I will give you the crown of life.	2:16	Repent therefore! Otherwise, I will soon come to you and will fight against them with the sword of my mouth.
APPEAL	2:7	He who has an ear, let him hear what the Spirit says to the churches.	2:11	He who has an ear, let him hear what the Spirit says to the churches.	2:17	He who has an ear, let him hear what the Spirit says to the churches.
ASSURANCE	2:7	To him who overcomes, I will give the right to eat from the tree of life, which is in the paradise of God.	2:11	He who overcomes will not be hurt at all by the second death.	2:17	To him who overcomes, I will give some of the hidden manna. I will also give him a white stone with a new name written on it, known only to him who receives it.

REVELATION TALK 2

REF	THYATIRA	REF	SARDIS	REF	PHILADELPHIA	REF	LAODICEA
2:18	To the angel of the church in Thyatira write:	3:1	To the angel of the church in Sardis write:	3:7	To the angel of the church in Philadelphia write:	3:14	To the angel of the church in Laodicea write:
2:18	These are the words of the Son of God, whose eyes are like blazing fire and whose feet are like burnished bronze.	3:1	These are the words of him who holds the seven spirits of God and the seven stars.	3:7	These are the words of him who is holy and true, who holds the key of David. What he opens no one can shut, and what he shuts no one can open.	3:14	These are the words of the Amen, the faithful and true witness, the ruler of God's creation.
2:19	I know your deeds, your love and faith, your service and perseverance, and that you are now doing more than you did at first.			3:8	I know your deeds. See, I have placed before you an open door that no one can shut. I know that you have little strength, yet you have kept my word and have not denied my name. I will make those		
				9	who are of the synagogue of Satan, who claim to be Jews though they are not, but are liars - I will make them come and fall down at your feet and acknowledge that I have		
				10	loved you. Since you have kept my command to endure patiently, I will also keep you from the hour of trial that is going to come upon the whole world to test those who live on the earth.		
2:20	Nevertheless, I have this against you: You tolerate that woman Jezebel, who calls herself a prophetess. By her teaching she misleads my servants into sexual immorality and the eating of food sacrificed to idols.	3:1	I know your deeds; you have a reputation of being alive, but you are dead. Wake up! Strengthen what remains and is about to die, for I have not found your deeds complete in the sight of my God.			3:15	I know your deeds, that you are neither cold nor hot. I wish you were either one or the other!
21	I have given her time to repent of her immorality, but she is	2				16	So, because you are lukewarm - neither hot nor cold - I am about to
22	unwilling. So I will cast her on a bed of suffering, and I will make those who commit adultery with her suffer intensely, unless they repent					17	spit you out of my mouth. You say, 'I am rich; I have acquired wealth and do not need a thing.' But you do not realise that you are
23	of her ways. I will strike her children dead. Then all the churches will know that I am he who searches hearts and minds, and I will repay each of you according to your deeds.						wretched, pitiful, poor, blind and naked.
						3:18	I counsel you to buy from me gold refined in the fire, so that you can become rich; and white clothes to wear, so that you can cover
2:24	Now I say to the rest of you in Thyatira, to you who do not hold to her teaching and have not learned Satan's so-called deep	3:3	Remember, therefore, what you have received and heard; obey it, and repent. But if you do not wake up, I will come like a thief, and you will not	3:11	I am coming soon. Hold on to what you have, so that no one will take your crown.		your shameful nakedness; and salve to put on your eyes, so that you can see.
25	secrets, (I will not impose any other burden on you), Only hold on to what you have until I come.	4	know at what time I will come to you. Yet you have a few people in Sardis who have not soiled their clothes. They will walk with me, dressed in white, for they are worthy.			19	Those whom I love I rebuke and discipline. So be earnest and repent.
						20	Here I am! I stand at the door and knock. If anyone hears my voice and opens the door, I will come in and eat with him, and he with me.
2:26	To him who overcomes and does my will to the end, I will give authority over	3:5	He who overcomes will, like them, be dressed in white. I will never blot out	3:12	Him who overcomes, I will make a pillar in the temple of my God. Never again will	3:21	To him who overcomes, I will give the right to sit with me on my throne,
27	the nations - He will rule them with an iron sceptre: he will dash them to pieces like pottery - just as I have		his name from the book of life, but will acknowledge his name before my Father and his angels.		he leave it. I will write on him the name of my God and the name of the city of my God, the new Jerusalem, which is		just as I overcame and sat down with my Father on his throne.
28	received authority from my Father. I will also give him the morning star.				coming down out of heaven from my God; and I will also write on him my new name.		
2:29	He who has an ear, let him hear what the Spirit says to the churches.	3:6	He who has an ear, let him hear what the Spirit says to the churches.	3:13	He who has an ear, let him hear what the Spirit says to the churches.	3:22	He who has an ear, let him hear what the Spirit says to the churches.

REVELATION TALK 2

LAODICEA

SEVEN CHURCHES OF ASIA

REVELATION TALK 2

PHILADELPHIA

SARDIS

REVELATION TALK 2

SMYRNA

EPHESUS

REVELATION TALK 2

THYATIRA

PERGAMUM

1. HEAVENLY CHRIST AND EARTHLY CHURCHES

2-3. THINGS ARE NOT ALRIGHT ON EARTH

CORRUPTED WORLD } *(IDOLATRY and IMMORALITY)*
COMPROMISED CHURCH

4-5. THINGS ARE ALRIGHT IN HEAVEN

GOD IS ON THE THRONE *(ALL OF HISTORY)*
JESUS IS IN CHARGE *(END OF HISTORY)*

6-18. THINGS WILL GET MUCH WORSE BEFORE THEY GET BETTER

FOR THE WORLD *WAR, BLOODSHED, FAMINE, DISEASE. NATURAL DISASTERS. MANY DEATHS.*
FOR THE CHURCH *BIG TROUBLE (3½ YEARS). UNHOLY TRINITY (SATAN, ANTICHRIST, FALSE PROPHET). CITY of BABYLON (PROSTITUTE). MANY DEATHS.*

19-22. THINGS WILL GET MUCH BETTER AFTER THEY GET WORSE

RETURN OF CHRIST TO EARTH *('FIRST' RESURRECTION)*
REIGN OF CHRIST ON EARTH *(1000 YEARS)*
DAY OF JUDGEMENT *('REST' RESURRECTION)*
SECOND DEATH *(LAKE OF FIRE)*
NEW HEAVEN AND EARTH
NEW JERUSALEM *(BRIDE)*

PHILOSOPHIES OF HISTORY

CYCLIC

PROGRESSIVE/ OPTIMISTIC

APOCALYPTIC
Jews
Christians } GOD
Communists - MAN

CONTINUOUS/EPIC

REGRESSIVE/ PESSIMISTIC

REVELATION TALK 3

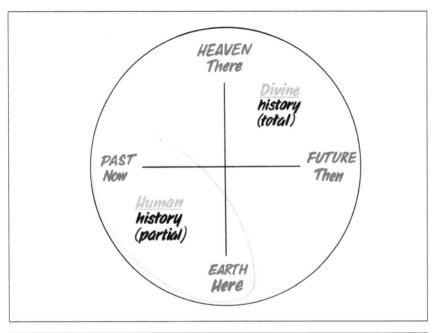

THREE SERIES OF 'SEVENS'

SEALS:
1. WHITE HORSE ~ AGGRESSION
2. RED HORSE ~ BLOODSHED
3. BLACK HORSE ~ FAMINE
4. GREEN HORSE ~ DISEASE

'WOES'
5. PERSECUTION & PRAYER (BELIEVERS)
6. TREMORS & TERROR (UNBELIEVERS)
7. SILENCE (EARTHQUAKE)

TRUMPETS:
1. SCORCHED EARTH
2. POLLUTED SEA
3. CONTAMINATED WATER
4. REDUCED SUNLIGHT

'WOES'
5. INSECT PLAGUE
6. ORIENTAL INVASION
7. KINGDOM COME (EARTHQUAKE)

BOWLS:
1. BOILS ON SKIN
2. BLOOD IN SEA
3. BLOOD FROM SPRINGS
4. BURNING BY SUN

'WOES'
5. DARKNESS
6. ARMAGEDDON
7. UNIVERSAL CATASTROPHE (EARTHQUAKE)

CHAPTERS 6-16

A. SUCCESSIVE

SEALS	TRUMPETS	BOWLS
1234567	1234567	1234567

B. SIMULTANEOUS

SEALS   1234567
TRUMPETS 1234567
BOWLS   1234567

C. SUCCESSIVE, SPEEDED, SIMULTANEOUS

SEALS   1   2   3   4-5   6   7
TRUMPETS   1 2 3 4-5 6   7
BOWLS   1234-567

Schools of interpretation:

PRETERIST ~ past (<u>first</u> century A.D.)
SEVEN HILLS OF ROME

HISTORICIST ~ present (<u>all</u> centuries A.D.)
SEVEN AGES OF THE CHURCH

FUTURIST ~ future (<u>last</u> century A.D.)
SEVEN YEARS OF GREAT TRIBULATION

IDEALIST ~ past present future (<u>any</u> century A.D.)
SEVEN NEW THINGS ALREADY

REVELATION TALK 4

WOMAN AND DRAGON — MICHAEL AND SATAN (COVENTRY)

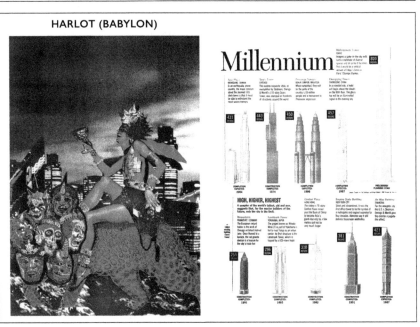

HARLOT (BABYLON)

REVELATION TALK 4

LATTER DAY BABYLON

FRANKFURT BANK PICTURE

FRANKFURT BANK STATUES

IMMINENCE – any moment?
(PRE-TRIBULATION 'RAPTURE')

1. STATEMENTS ABOUT SPEED
   I AM COMING SOON, QUICKLY.

2. STATEMENTS ABOUT SURPRISE
   THIEF IN THE NIGHT: YOU KNOW NOT.

3. DIFFERENCES OF LANGUAGE
   DAY OF LORD / DAY OF CHRIST
   ARRIVAL / APPEARING
   FOR SAINTS / WITH SAINTS

4. EXPECTATION OF THE CHURCH
   HE IS AT THE DOOR
   THIS GENERATION WILL NOT PASS AWAY.

5. ABSENCE OF 'CHURCH' (in tribulation passages)
   ELECT, SAINTS

6. EMPHASIS ON COMFORT
   ENCOURAGE ONE ANOTHER

7. TRIBULATION IS 'WRATH'
   GOD DID NOT APPOINT US TO WRATH.

REVELATION TALK 5

SEVEN VISIONS ('and I saw')

1. <u>PAROUSIA</u> (19. *11-16*)   KING OF KINGS, LORD OF LORDS.
'LOGOS' = WORD
WHITE HORSE, BLOODSTAINED ROBE

2. <u>SUPPER</u> (19. *17-18*)   ANGELS INVITE BIRDS...
...TO GORGE ON CORPSES.

3. <u>ARMAGEDDON</u> (19. *19-21*)   KINGS AND ARMIES DESTROYED
BY 'WORD' = LOGOS
BEAST AND FALSE PROPHET INTO LAKE OF FIRE.

4. <u>SATAN</u> (20. *1-3*)   BOUND AND BANISHED TO 'ABYSS'
BUT FOR LIMITED TIME.

5. <u>MILLENNIUM</u> (20. *4-10*)   SAINTS AND MARTYRS REIGN
FIRST RESURRECTION
SATAN RELEASED, INTO LAKE OF FIRE.

6. <u>JUDGEMENT</u> (20. *11-15*)   RESURRECTION OF 'THE 'REST'
BOOKS AND 'BOOK OF LIFE' OPENED.

7. <u>RE-CREATION</u> (21. *1-2*)   NEW HEAVEN AND EARTH
NEW JERUSALEM.

REVELATION TALK 5

HILL OF MEGIDDO - ARMAGEDDON

1. <u>A-MILLENNIAL</u> (better <u>non</u>-mill)

a. SCEPTICAL
       Absurdity
b. MYTHOLOGICAL
       Allegory

2. <u>POST-MILLENNIAL</u> (Christ returns <u>after</u>)

a. SPIRITUAL
       Whole church age
b. POLITICAL
       Last part church age

3. <u>PRE-MILLENNIAL</u> (Christ returns <u>before</u>)

a. DISPENSATIONAL
       Israel
b. CLASSICAL
       Church

REVELATION TALK 5

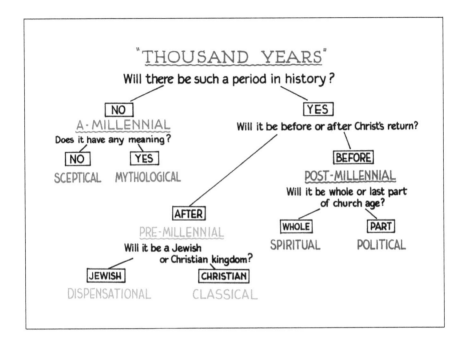

REVELATION TALK 6

SEVEN VISIONS ('and I <u>saw</u>')

1. <u>PAROUSIA</u> (19. *11-16*)   KING OF KINGS, LORD OF LORDS.
'LOGOS' = WORD
WHITE HORSE, BLOODSTAINED ROBE

2. <u>SUPPER</u> (19. *17-18*)   ANGELS INVITE BIRDS...
...TO GORGE ON CORPSES.

3. <u>ARMAGEDDON</u> (19. *19-21*)   KINGS AND ARMIES DESTROYED
BY 'WORD' = LOGOS
BEAST AND FALSE PROPHET INTO LAKE OF FIRE.

4. <u>SATAN</u> (20. *1-3*)   BOUND AND BANISHED TO 'ABYSS'
BUT FOR LIMITED TIME.

5. <u>MILLENNIUM</u> (20. *4-10*)   SAINTS AND MARTYRS REIGN
FIRST RESURRECTION
SATAN RELEASED, INTO LAKE OF FIRE.

6. <u>JUDGEMENT</u> (20. *11-15*)   RESURRECTION OF 'THE 'REST'
BOOKS AND 'BOOK OF LIFE' OPENED.

7. <u>RE-CREATION</u> (21. *1-2*)   NEW HEAVEN AND EARTH
NEW JERUSALEM.

STONES OF NEW JERUSALEM

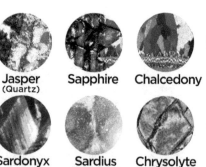

Jasper (Quartz)   Sapphire   Chalcedony   Emerald

Sardonyx   Sardius (Carnelian)   Chrysolyte (Peridot)   Beryl (Aquamarine)

Topaz   Chrysoprasus   Jacinth (Zircon)   Amethyst

REVELATION TALK 6

STONES REJECTED

Diamond   Spinal   Pyrope   Alamandine

MT. ETNA (LAKE OF FIRE)

REVELATION TALK 6

WHY STUDY "REVELATION"?

1. COMPLETION of BIBLE
2. DEFENCE AGAINST HERESY
3. INTERPRETATION of HISTORY
4. GROUND for HOPE
5. MOTIVE for EVANGELISM
6. STIMULUS to WORSHIP
7. ANTIDOTE to WORLDLINESS
8. INCENTIVE to GODLINESS
9. PREPARATION for PERSECUTION
10. UNDERSTANDING of CHRIST

Printed in the USA
CPSIA information can be obtained
at www.ICGtesting.com
LVHW011956010224
770619LV00003B/510